180 INSPIRATIONS TO START A TEACHER'S DAY

Before the
BELL RINGS

VICKI CARUANA

BESTSELLING AUTHOR OF *Apples and Chalkdust*

HOWARD BOOKS
A DIVISION OF SIMON & SCHUSTER

NEW YORK LONDON TORONTO SIDNEY

Our purpose at Howard Books is to:
- *Increase faith* in the hearts of growing Christians
- *Inspire holiness* in the lives of believers
- *Instill hope* in the hearts of struggling people everywhere

Because He's coming again!

Published by Howard Books, a division of Simon & Schuster
1230 Avenue of the Americas, New York, NY 10020
www.howardpublishing.com

Before the Bell Rings © 2006 by Vicki Caruana

ISBN 10: 1-4165-3590-X; ISBN 13: 978-1-4165-3590-4
ISBN 10: 1-58229-571-9; ISBN 13: 978-1-58229-571-8

10   9   8   7   6   5   4   3   2

HOWARD colophon is a registered trademark of Simon & Schuster, Inc.

Manufactured in China

For information regarding special discounts for bulk purchases, please contact Simon & Schuster Special Sales at 1-800-456-6798 or business@simonandschuster.com.

Edited by Rachelle Gardner
Interior design by John Mark Luke Designs
Cover design by Design Works

*To the education majors of the graduating
class of 2005 from St. Petersburg College*

GO FORTH AND LET YOUR LIGHT SHINE!

ACKNOWLEDGMENTS

I'd like to thank the folks at Howard Books who recognized the daily needs of teachers by the inception of this book and then choosing to run with it. I'd also like to thank my editor and friend, Rachelle Gardner, for both expertly and lovingly meshing my words and insights into the hearts of teachers in a way that makes a difference.

GOOD MORNING!

It's the start of a new school year! Maybe it's your first; maybe it's your last. No matter how many years you've been teaching, I know there are times you feel alone, oh so weary, and even skeptical that any good can come from the school year just beginning to come into view. As someone who's been there and knows what your life is like, allow me the privilege to minister to you day by day over the course of this school year. Before the kids burst into your classroom, and before the demands of the day arm-wrestle you to the ground, sit in the presence of the only thing that brings rest and refreshment—the Word of God— coupled with the understanding of a friend. Set aside just a few minutes each day, before the bell rings!

I hope you will gain more than insight and understanding from the daily readings in this book. I hope you will feel both encouraged and empowered to reach out to other teachers in your midst and minister to them as well. After all, who better knows what a teacher's life is like than another teacher?

For more information, support and encouragement, visit us online at www.vickicaruana.blogspot.com.

*Be imitators of God, as dearly loved
children. And walk in love, as the Messiah also
loved us and gave Himself for us,
a sacrificial and fragrant offering to God.*

EPHESIANS 5:1–2

THE SMELL OF SUCCESS

What does the first day of school smell like? Close
your eyes and take a whiff. The delightful mix of
freshly painted walls, cleaning supplies, and maybe
even new carpet fills the senses. There's only one in-
gredient missing—the fragrance of children.

You've set up your supplies, organized the textbooks on their shelves, and entered this year's students into your class roll book. Nothing is missing;
nothing is broken; you have enough of everything—
for now. For a brief instant you survey your sur-
roundings with a definite sense of satisfaction. To
begin again is always a good thing. You take a deep
cleansing breath and open your classroom door.

Your moment of peace is shattered by children
pushing their way past you to take their first look at

their new home for the next ten months. You catch their scent as they wiggle around you like a school of fish. New backpacks, new clothes, freshly shampooed hair, and brushed teeth. Before long your room will lose its new-school-year smell. Today is the best it will smell all year. But even when the carpet no longer smells fresh (nor do the children, for that matter), one subtle scent remains—the fragrance of hope. That's something children can smell a mile away. Like hungry travelers homing in on a freshly baked apple pie, they'll follow that delicious scent right to you!

FINAL THOUGHT: Does your aroma attract followers? Let the perfume of hope permeate your pores.

My Lord, I follow Your scent toward the promise of new life. Let my aroma, in turn, be a sweet invitation to students when they walk into my classroom. Bless me with their enthusiasm and even their anxiety so that I might know what they need.

Day 2

Then we will no longer be little children, tossed by the waves and blown around by every wind of teaching, by human cunning with cleverness in the techniques of deceit.

HERE TODAY, GONE TOMORROW

One thing you can count on as a teacher is that nothing stays the same. Just when you think you've got it all figured out, the situation changes. Remember the paperwork you had to complete last year to track student literacy progress? Well, it's different this year. Remember the committee reports you had to file in triplicate? They did away with them. Remember those three state testing days you had in October? Now there are five. And by the way, the cafeteria will no longer serve that chicken caesar salad you loved and bought every Thursday. It's Taco Thursday now.

There are a few things that never change, though. You will rewrite your class roll at least twice during the first twenty days of school. Something will be missing from your supply order. And the little darling who drives you the craziest will never be absent! Hopefully you started this school year with a measure of enthusiasm, and hopefully that will never change.

Fads filter into our schools every year. Sometimes they show up in the clothing choices of our students. Other times it's the reading or math approach. Most often it's educational-reform attempts. The winds of change whip around us, threatening to dismantle any progress we've made. But when we hold on to absolutes—the love of Christ and the truth of the gospel—we can stand firm. We can thank God for the gifts that brought us to teaching in the first place—a love for children and a strong desire to make a difference. Then we can withstand the tossing and turning of policies, parents, and politicians.

FINAL THOUGHT: Seasons change, programs change, budgets change—but none of that has to change our love of God and our love of teaching.

Lord, in this ever-changing world You are the only constant. Thank You for Your immutable character that encourages me to focus on the truth of the gospel that never alters.

DAY 3

Rejoice with those who rejoice;
weep with those who weep.

ROMANS 12:15

CONTAGIOUS ENTHUSIASM

We all begin the school year with excitement, even if things don't start out the way we expected. You might have been surprised to discover you were moved into a portable classroom over the summer. You may be wondering where the other science teacher is, only to find out his unit was cut and he's now at another school. Yet there's still excitement on the first days of school. Even after a decade of teaching first grade, you giggle at the sight of those little ones looking for their nametags taped to their very own desks.

You may have spent years fine-tuning your program and teaching strategies. You might have logged hundreds and hundreds of days learning the rules, following the rules, and enforcing the rules. You know every student trick in the book to get out of doing homework. Nothing seems new to you any-more, but—surprise! Your students are excited at the beginning of the school year. Some may not show it, but there's joy, fear, trepidation, silliness, awe, and even anxiety all bundled together and running deep like a strong ocean current. To them it is all new. It's their first time in first, second, fourth, or twelfth grade.

We can catch their wave of excitement if we choose to. We can get into the water with them and body-surf to the beach instead of sitting on the shore waiting for our charges to wear themselves out. We can be eager and energized together, and then later we can all be exhausted together!

 FINAL THOUGHT: We can intentionally experience the novelty of school through our students' eyes if we jump in and participate in their excitement.

May my desire always be to offer You the first fruits of my labor. Lord, let me be caught up in the excitement of these first days of school.

DAY 4

But the fruit of the Spirit is love, joy, peace, patience, kindness, goodness, faith, gentleness, self-control.

GALATIANS 5:22–23

NAME TAGS

Some of us are better than others at remembering names. Every year, sometimes twice a year, you have a list of names to memorize as quickly as possible. Nothing is worse than being forgotten or over-looked, so those first tenuous days of the school year challenge you to commit to memory anywhere between 20 and 150 student names. Making nametags on the first day of school is a common practice. But the real names seem to fade in favor of the ones we assign.

Fidgety. Clown. Late. Talks too much. Painfully shy. Really smart. Really not. Popular. Charming. Might be a problem. You know the unwritten names you assign your students during those first days and weeks. Believe it or not, they facilitate the remembering of their given names. It's those who don't catch your attention quickly enough, and therefore

go without your private naming, that you'll forget—
or not even learn their names in the first place.

Unnoticed. Unobtrusive. Unremarkable. You
learn their names last. If they raise their hands,
you pause just long enough for them to realize you
don't remember. They know their unspoken needs
are easily forgotten.

Yet these are the ones who need us the most.
They're the ones whose quiet existence pales in con-
trast to the aggressive outpourings of their peers.
They need your attention. They need your praise.
And they need you to know their names—right
away.

FINAL THOUGHT: What are the unspoken names your students assign to
you? When the fruit of the Spirit shines
through, your names will be *Patience*,
Kindness, *Goodness*, and *Gentleness*.

*Lord, Yours is the Name above every
name. One day every tongue will con-
fess that You are Lord. Help me to know
Your names and bestow only names on
Your children that are honorable and
worthy of praise.*

9

*Now faith is the reality of what is hoped for,
the proof of what is not seen.*

HEBREWS 11:1

A LONG SHOT

How are you at picking winners? Are your powers of predictability accurate? When you survey your classroom, what do you see? As a veteran teacher you recognize the Hard-Working Harrys, the Lazy Larrys, the Focused Fionas, and the Barely-Getting-By Beckys. You can tell within the first few weeks who will succeed and who will not. But this is a pretty high-stakes game. How much are you willing to bet on your yet unproven colts?

It doesn't even matter how they ran the previous races. What matters is this one—this year. Giacomo, a California-based colt, won the 2005 Kentucky Derby at 50-1 odds. He hadn't won any of his previous races that year until that Saturday. He'd made small strides forward with each start, building toward the ultimate goal of the Derby. Even an untried horse has a chance to take home the winning cup.

Safe bets are just that—safe. When we put our energies into something we know will succeed, any perceived risk is minimized. Betting on a long shot threatens failure, a diminished reputation, and in schools, possibly a loss of funding. On the other hand, putting your money on a long shot can offer the greatest reward. Just ask anyone who bet on Giacomo.

Students can surprise us. They can come from behind and run those last yards nose to nose with the best and the brightest, finally winning in a photo finish! If we refuse to prejudge and, instead, let each one show us what they've got, we allow them the opportunity to run their best race ever.

FINAL THOUGHT: Slow and steady starters often have what it takes to win in the end—our faith in them can make the difference.

Lord, let me always be mindful that my faith in students may be what draws them to You.

11

DAY 6

Be diligent to present yourself approved to God,
a worker who doesn't need to be ashamed,
correctly teaching the word of truth.

2 TIMOTHY 2:15

LEARNING CURVE

Continual learning is a trademark of good teaching. There will undoubtedly be some new things for you to learn this year. Whether it's new curriculum, new procedures, or new colleagues, there's always something unfamiliar to master. Sometimes you get the chance to prepare over the summer for the coming year's changes. Other times it surprises you like a baby left on your doorstep, and you have no choice but to embrace it and learn how to care for it.

Preparedness is preferred, but even when you're faced with teaching from a new text or you've been assigned a new subject area, or suddenly you're expected to team teach with someone you barely know, everything you've done so far has prepared you for what you're about to do.

One of the tools with which God has equipped

you is the desire to learn. That willingness alone will offer you both insight and expertise into areas that right now baffle and befuddle you.

God equips those He calls. It's no coincidence that you've had to learn to pay attention to and devise ways to meet the needs of many different children—other people's children. Flexible and creative thinking helps you solve new problems every day. Even when you happen upon new and unforeseen challenges, this is the work uniquely prepared for your hands. If you feel inadequate or ill-prepared, you can still be sure that God has you exactly where He needs you to be.

FINAL THOUGHT: We don't need to be insecure about what we don't know. We are always able to learn something new.

Help prepare my heart to believe Your Word. Help my mind to meditate on Your principles. Help my hands to do the work prepared for them—each and every day.

DAY 7

*Don't work for the food that perishes
but for the food that lasts for eternal life,
which the Son of Man will give you, because God the
Father has set His seal of approval on Him.*

JOHN 6:27

WITH THE END IN MIND

It's hard not to feel like you're teaching to the test when you're told that your job is to ensure good test results. Lately some districts have started school earlier in the year to get a jump on the fall testing. Some of us have a weekly schedule that includes teaching test-taking skills. Teacher training frequently focuses on nutrition for optimal performance, preventing test anxiety, and ensuring valid and reliable test results. Sometimes it feels like we're being set up for failure.

Yet lawyers have bar exams to pass if they are to be considered competent and able to practice law. Even with professors' individual nuances, I'm sure they ultimately teach to the test. Doctors are expected to meet layers upon layers of standards, in-

14

cluding learning how to practice medicine on little to no sleep. Even firemen and policemen have exams to pass and physical, emotional, and mental challenges to overcome if they are going to meet standards. We wouldn't want it any other way. Testing serves a crucial purpose in numerous walks of life, and test results can be meaningful if interpreted and utilized properly.

Even if we question the accountability measures behind state testing, we can still succeed by doing our jobs to the best of our ability. We can teach what is required, while always remembering the goal of growing dependent children into competent adults. If we want our students to be successful, productive, and happy, it will help to keep this end in mind as we teach.

FINAL THOUGHT: If we do our jobs well, our students will do well, no matter the test.

Lord, help me to focus on the eternal. Even when a test or trial threatens to steal my hope, help me to remember that my hope lies in the promise of what is still to come.

Share with the saints in their needs; pursue hospitality.

ROMANS 12:13

WHEN YOU KNOW TOO MUCH

We start the year with more information about our students than we should. Their cumulative folders are handed over to us, and what's inside rivals an FBI file. We know whose parents are divorced; who's on medication; who's been left back, accelerated, or homeschooled; who has moved every other year; is on free or reduced lunch; has parents in the military; is adopted; speaks very little English; has emotional or behavioral problems; needs special education; is in danger of dropping out—and we know their IQs.

They say information is power. Then why is it that even though we know all about our students, we still feel powerless? Maybe ignorance really is bliss. We'd certainly have less to worry about, and in reality we'd have less to be accountable for. But there's a reason you know that Jessica's parents just divorced; there's a reason why you're told that Chad has always struggled in math.

16

The insider information we've been given can be used for good. We can hold these precious and sometimes private insights as carefully as we would a baby bird with a broken wing, cupped with a generous insulation of grace. Maybe these flashes of insight remind you of your own struggles and shortcomings. Maybe you can now breathe relevance into your teaching in a way you could not have before. We can connect with students on a deeper level. We know what we know for a reason, and that reason is always for God's good purposes.

 FINAL THOUGHT: Even when you think you know too much, remember you still have a lot to learn.

Lord, speak Your wisdom into my heart. Reveal to me the hidden needs of my students so that I may better serve them.

DAY 9

*If the watchman sees the sword coming but doesn't blow
the trumpet, so that the people aren't warned, and the
sword comes and takes away their lives, then
they have been taken away because of their iniquity, but I
will hold the watchman accountable for their blood.*

EZEKIEL 33:6

DUTY FREE

At this point you know what your extra duties are
in your school. The duty roster has been posted, and
you know where you're supposed to be and when.
Whether it's on the bus ramp, the hallway, the playground, at the front entrance, or in the lunch room,
everyone counts on your vigilance.

Yes, these duties take away from precious moments in your classroom—time you never feel like
you get back. It's frustrating to stand outside alone
when you know Mr. or Mrs. So-and-So is supposed
to be out there as well. Doing the right thing is never
easy, especially when some of your colleagues choose
to ignore their obligations. As much as we groan and
complain about our extra assignments, whether it's

to watch the hallways, sponsor school clubs, or mentor students after school, their purposes outweigh our inconvenience.

These duties make us more visible to students. The more they see us, the more they'll get to know us. The more they get to know us, the more they can trust us enough to learn from us. The faithful fulfillment of even the smallest of duties goes a long way to communicate to staff and students that you care about your job as an educator. The Boy Scout pledge says, "On my honor I will do my best to do my duty to God and my country . . ." We can find contentment with even our most distasteful duties when we make *honor* the key characteristic of how we perform them. We honor our commitments, our students, and most importantly, our God when we accept duties without protest and with praise to the Father who enables us to do them.

FINAL THOUGHT: Not only are you watching your students, but they are watching you.

Lord, enable me to follow the path of righteousness, even when I'm weary, even when I don't want to, and even when no one else does.

Go, therefore, and make disciples of all nations,
baptizing them in the name of the Father and
of the Son and of the Holy Spirit.

MATTHEW 28:19

MINI ME

Most people who go into teaching loved school. Even if they themselves struggled through algebra or creative writing, there was one teacher who encouraged them enough that they are driven to give that very encouragement to another mathphobic or sentence-challenged youngster. Personally, I just loved learning and couldn't wait each day for my next mouthful of meaning, savoring each morsel as mindfully as a connoisseur of gourmet food. For whatever reason you went into teaching, you have a picture of the perfect student in your mind. And if you're like most of us, you hope your students will be just like you.

They'll study the way you studied. They'll behave the way you behaved. They'll love learning like you loved it. Even if it took you until now to become the model student, you want your young scholars to be just like you right now. The corollary of this desire is that you teach the way you like to be taught, and you relate the way you like to relate.

Making disciples out of students requires us to step back from our natural yearning for little look-alikes. If we make the effort to really see who they are and become what they need, they will be empowered to become who they are meant to be. Paul said, "I have become all things to all people, so that I may by all means save some" (1 Corinthians 9:22). It's not about replicating ourselves in our students, but it's a matter of facilitating their success by being exactly the teacher each student needs. With God's help we can become all things to all students, knowing they won't all succeed but that we're doing everything we can to provide the opportunity.

FINAL THOUGHT: As flattering as it is that your students may want to grow up to be just like you, point them instead to become like the One you hope to mimic every day.

Heavenly Father, my greatest desire is to learn to be just like You, so that when my students look at me, they only see You!

For the desire to do what is good is with me, but there is no ability to do it. For I do not do the good that I want to do, but I practice the evil that I do not want to do.

ROMANS 7:18–19

I SPY

Do you see what I see? I spy a beautiful, blonde-haired maiden sitting by herself on the playground. Do you see what I see? I spy a little boy wearing the same clothes day after day. Do you see what I see? I spy a gaggle of girls whispering and laughing about another little girl. Do you see what I see? I spy no other teacher in the hallway but me between classes.

There's so much that escapes our notice during the school day, but there is so much more that we *do* see and find ourselves doing nothing about. We operate with two to-do lists: the visible one that lists all the practical have-to's of our days, and the invisible one that lists all the shoulds of our days. I should call Sam's mother and find out why he wears the same clothes every day. I should invite my new-

22

est student to eat lunch with me so she doesn't sit on the playground alone. I should stop that gang of girls from teasing poor Mary. I should remind my colleague that I can't manage the hallways by myself between classes.

We shy away from the shoulds because their outcomes don't seem so certain. There's a chance things won't change, or they might even get worse. But in reality the shoulds make our have-to's more manageable. Intervening now, before things get out of hand, saves us time later spent filling out disciplinary referrals, anecdotal accounts for the social worker or school psychologist, or conference notes typed up in triplicate for an irate parent. We can do what's expected of us, not just because someone says we should, but because it's the right thing to do. Any good we do comes out of God's abundance, not our ability.

FINAL THOUGHT: Try each day to do more than see; do something about what you see.

Lord, open the eyes of my heart, and let me see what You see. Then equip me to do something about it.

*My dear brothers, be steadfast, immovable, always
excelling in the Lord's work, knowing that
your labor in the Lord is not in vain.*

I CORINTHIANS 15:58

RED LIGHT, GREEN LIGHT, 1, 2, 3

Did you have some grand plans that just aren't coming together the way you'd hoped this year? Maybe
you planned an incredible unit on the Great White
Way, knowing your community theater would be
putting on four classic Broadway plays, only to discover there's a moratorium on field trips. Maybe you
gathered enough pen pals in a Middle Eastern country for all of your students just when the civil mail
service there fell apart. These aren't little things—
they were long-term projects with high interest and
high impact. And now you have to go back to the
drawing board and start again.

Enthusiasm wanes when the best-laid plans dis-
appear in the dust. The energy it took to determine
and develop those dreams was so intense that the
thought of replicating the effort makes you want to

lie down until the feeling passes. But success only comes with forward movement, and if that means two steps forward and one step back, over time you will still find yourself ahead. Even if your original plans were thwarted by a hard-to-control class, un-appreciative parents, unsupportive administrators, or other circumstances beyond your control, find a Plan B, and put it into effect. Put one foot in front of the other and keep walking.

FINAL THOUGHT: Any forward movement, even with stops and starts, is still progress.

Lord, help me to patiently walk with perseverance in the path You set at my feet.

We all, with unveiled faces, are reflecting the glory of the Lord and are being transformed into the same image from glory to glory; this is from the Lord who is the Spirit.

2 Corinthians 3:18

Picture Day

It's time yet again to sit on those terribly uncomfortable little stools with our knees pointed to the right, our shoulders square to the camera, our hands in our laps, left over right, and our chins tilted ever so slightly to one side (whichever side the photographer deems is our better one—not that they really know). School-picture day is here. The pained expressions in the photos of some teachers reveal that the promise of an 8 x 10 and twenty wallet-sized photos is completely lost on them. Personally, I have yet to find twenty people to send those wallets to.

These photos taken at the beginning of the school year—before the weariness set in, before your supplies ran out, and before problem students and problem parents tested your patience—represent you for the year. It's the same face that will grace the pages of the yearbook and remind students long after the year is over who you were to them.

Allow the image caught on film to reflect your enthusiasm and the hope you have at the beginning of the year. Approach picture day with the purpose of putting your best face forward. Remember in Whose image you were created, and let that light shine through. Live each day so that the character revealed in your photo matches the character that is evident throughout the year to all who come in contact with you.

FINAL THOUGHT: What we do today determines how we will be remembered later.

Lord, let my countenance reveal the hope that is within me!

Better one handful with rest, than two handfuls with effort and pursuit of the wind.

ECCLESIASTES 4:6

GIVE ME A BREAK!

Does the teachers lounge beckon you like the ancient sirens of the Aegean Sea? Does it promise respite, retreat, and relaxation if you just quietly wander in when you should be on hall duty or grading last-minute spelling tests? The allure is most captivating when the lounge is empty and there's nothing between you, a cup of coffee, and that candy machine. The decrepit, threadbare couch has seen better days, but then again, so have you. You plop down on it and breathe a well-deserved sigh of relief—for about thirty seconds.

You're not the only weary traveler who's intent on finding some spot of tranquility amidst the sometimes deafening demands of students, parents, and fellow teachers. Others who drift into the teachers' lounge are looking for that same five minutes of peace and quiet. It's the only place students and parents can't invade and where the savoring of one square of a chocolate bar, a few sips of coffee, or a moment of adult conversation seem like heaven on earth. Even a moment of rest is better than rushing around all day every day with your hands full of work and never any calm. These opportunities, as worldly as they seem, beckon you into God's rest—created by Him especially for you. Be thankful and enjoy them when you can.

FINAL THOUGHT: Try to write "rest" into your daily lesson plans.

Lord, help me to be aware of those pockets of rest You created just for me, even when they don't look like I expect them to.

A wise man will listen and increase his learning.

PROVERBS 1:5

GETTING TO KNOW YOU

The more you know, the better able you will be to teach. One of the most productive things you can do at the beginning of the school year is to listen. We do so much talking as teachers that it's hard to quiet ourselves long enough to hear the wails of the frustrated, the whimpers of the defeated, or the sighs of the bored in our midst. It's like learning the cries of your newborn and trying to figure out if he's hungry, wet, tired, hurting, frustrated, or scared. After a while you can recognize which cries require your immediate attention and which do not.

Some students don't even make a sound to catch your attention. How can you get to know them if they don't say a word? My cat doesn't speak, but I can sure tell what's going on with her. Lying on the couch sprawled out means she's relaxed and feels safe. Hiding under a bed means she's overwhelmed.

Tail swishing back and forth and pupils large means she's feisty and ready to pounce.

We're all familiar with the ways both verbal and body language speak to us. What matters is if we're actually listening. As your students wander into your room today, watch and listen to what they're telling you about what they need.

FINAL THOUGHT: Listen today as if you are eavesdropping on someone— listening for information you can use to your advantage. Then find a way to use what you hear to impact the lives of your students.

Lord, enhance all the senses You've created me with so that I may see what's not visible and hear what no one actually says.

Trust in the LORD with all your heart,
and do not rely on your own understanding;
think about Him in all your ways,
and He will guide you on the right paths.

PROVERBS 3:5–6

I DON'T GET IT

Why is it that when we teach the unit to the best of our ability, half of our students still fail the test? Why is it that when we send home class newsletters, e-mail reminders to every parent, and conduct individual conferences, some parents still act surprised when we penalize their child for not completing the science project on time? And why is it that even when we stack the chairs, pick up the big stuff, and clear the desktops, the custodian still gets annoyed with us? I don't get it! Do you? It seems that even when we do all that we're supposed to do, things go wrong, people aren't satisfied, and fingers are pointed our way.

The school year is still in its infancy, and already some things feel out of our control. Parents are complaining, colleagues are frustrated, and the principal's demands seem out of touch and unrealistic. Our "expert" status as teachers can get us into trouble. We begin to rely on it and expect to be able to solve every problem.

It's time to make some choices. When you find yourself asking why things are going the way they are, see it as an opportunity to relinquish your desire to find the answers. Decide which situations are within your control, focus on those, and let the rest go. Even students need to focus on what they can do instead of what they can't do. There is a time to walk forward boldly and a time to ask for help.

Sometimes we have to get ourselves out of God's way. We can and must do our due diligence, but God is ultimately responsible for the outcome. We can trust Him to deliver.

FINAL THOUGHT: Self-reliance leads to unrest. God-reliance is the only way to peace.

Heavenly Father, thank You for always being on Your throne and in control. You hold the universe together, so I know You can hold my life together.

Whoever sows contempt for his neighbor lacks sense,
but a man with understanding keeps silent.

PROVERBS 11:12

PARTNERS IN WHINE

Schools are communities, and communities are collections of neighbors. What happens when you don't get along with your neighbors? Sometimes they borrow things but never return them. Sometimes they're noisy. Sometimes they gossip, or their manners are questionable. Often our reaction to unlovable neighbors is to avoid them. But that's only possible to a certain extent within a school.

Are you sitting in your classroom right now knowing you have trouble with one of your colleagues? Maybe you avoid her, or perhaps you've discovered you can bridge the gap by adopting a common issue to complain about. Neighbors who don't really relish each other's company often come to a meeting of the minds when they complain about the inefficiency of the garbageman or how late the mailman comes each day. School "neighbors" tend to complain in unison about the unrealistic demands of an administrator or the unruly parent they both deal with.

A den of complaint is not a safe place, and it fosters disharmony. Is there a way to build bridges without tearing someone else down? We can choose to disengage from the gossip and whining, and instead, pray for those colleagues who drive us crazy. We can actively search for common ground that doesn't involve grumbling. Jesus said, "Blessed are the peacemakers" (Matthew 5:9), for situations such as this. We can try to be a part of the solution and never a part of the problem. Even if the complaints are valid, we can offer understanding with prayerful silence instead of nonsensical noise.

FINAL THOUGHT: Love your neighbor —that's the bottom line.

God, I know You expect me to love those most unlovable, but I don't know how. Show me how, and until I can, please love them through me.

Arrogance leads to nothing but strife,
but wisdom is gained by those who take advice.

PROVERBS 13:10

TALK TO THE HAND!

None of us knows it all. Even someone with twenty-years experience in the classroom regularly faces a need to learn something new or do something differently. Procedures change. Programs change. Policies change. Even the smallest detail, when altered, can make us feel like our territory has been invaded and our boundaries breached. How do you react when things change, when doing things the way you've always done them is no longer acceptable? Do you bristle and try to bully your way around the new expectations?

This is my class. These are my kids. This is the way I do things. I hate technology. Staff development is a waste of my time. Administrators don't know what it's like in a classroom nowadays. If it adds one more thing to my day, I won't do it. Sound familiar? The territorial nature of many teachers makes it difficult for others to extend a hand in friendship or encouragement. And this attitude in us leads down the road of arrogance to a place of apathy and, eventually, irrelevance.

Is there something going on in your school that has your feathers ruffled? Have you been asked to do something you'd rather not do? Did someone suggest you might want to change how you teach, how you interact with students or parents, or how you manage paperwork?

Drop your defenses. Say good-bye to arrogance and good riddance to rigidity. Smile and do your best to hear the helpful message being offered, even if it means letting go of some long-held and comfortable ways of doing things.

FINAL THOUGHT: That hand of advice is not there to slap you but to encourage you. Try not to bite it!

Lord, I've allowed my pride to cloud my judgment. Forgive me and then humble me so that I may be the effective teacher You've called me to be.

There is profit in all hard work,
but endless talk leads only to poverty.

PROVERBS 14:23

ALL TALK AND NO ACTION

What stands in the way of satisfaction in your work? What needs to happen in order for you to feel good about teaching every day? What obstacles threaten to derail you from your quest? Sometimes it's as simple as your own choices. If you feel stuck, maybe it's because you choose not to move. If you feel trapped, perhaps you are refusing to escape. If you feel bored, have you thought about changing the way you do things?

When I'm feeling dissatisfied or blocked, I like to think of water as my inspiration. All water is on a mission to return to the sea, and water always finds a way. From the roar of Niagara Falls to the dripping faucet keeping you up at night, water looks for the path of least resistance on its way home. That path doesn't equate with ease or inconsequence. It was water that carved out the Grand Canyon. It was water that created caves and caverns and rocky coastlines and beautiful sandy beaches under our feet. Water rarely stops moving. Even when we try to tame it, it breaks through. Holding back the tide is a risky proposition at best.

Instead of looking at a colleague who just got her master's degree and thinking *I wish I could do that*, find a way! When you hear about a teacher who received a grant that made her program more effective than ever, don't just think *I wish someone would give me a grant*. Make it happen! These are opportunities to think about where we are, where we want to be, and how to get there. We are where we choose to be.

FINAL THOUGHT: We can always make a different choice.

Lord, Your greatest gift to mankind is free will. I am always free to choose, but I would love Your counsel as I do so.

*A person who is full tramples on a honeycomb,
but to a hungry person, any bitter thing is sweet.*

PROVERBS 27:7

LEFTOVERS

Schools usually seem to be in either feast or famine, never in-between. For those of us who operate on miniscule and shrinking budgets, we feel as if we're sifting through rubble like those who've lost their homes to a tornado, scouring the debris for anything precious or at least good enough to keep. We'll retrieve one shoe or one fork or one dish out of the ashes, believing that one day we'll find its match and be fully functional again. We believe in the possibilities. We are always hungry.

Those of us for whom cutbacks are rare and coffers overflow tend to discard those things that *aren't just right* or *don't quite fit*. If we want poster board, we get poster board (not newsprint). If we want enough texts for each student, we get them (instead of just one class set). If we want each student to have his or her own Spanish verbs dictionary, we provide them (rather than asking parents to buy them). If we have a bursting budget, we spend every penny (even if we don't need to). We bask in our current financial status. We are never hungry.

There is nothing noble about being hungry; there is nothing less spiritual about being full. Our attitude reveals where the treasures of our heart really lie. Look around your classroom today. What do you have that you can share? Moving beyond classroom needs, is there someone hungrier than you with whom you can share a kind word, an understanding hug? To whom can you show compassion? To whom can you extend mercy? By the time you get to heaven, your storehouses can be full if you find ways to give what someone else needs today—no matter the size of your annual budget.

FINAL THOUGHT: No matter how much or how little we're given, we can pass it on.

Lord, You know the desires of my heart. Help me to distinguish between need and desire so that I can rest in the fact that You will provide for my needs. Show me ways I can share with others.

Don't [work only] while being watched, in order to please men, but as slaves of Christ, do God's will from your heart.

EPHESIANS 6:6

GOOD ENOUGH TO GET BY

"What do I need to do to pass?" Sound familiar? Students ask this all the time, but more and more teachers want to know the answer as well.

"How many in-service points do I need this year?"

"How many of my students need to pass the exam in order for us to retain our school rating?"

"How many one-on-one parent conferences must I hold in order to meet the parent-involvement component of our school-improvement plan?"

"How many sick days can I take before my principal gets annoyed?"

We spend so much time checking on whether or not we're meeting the minimum standards. Have we forgotten that those guidelines are to remind us of the *least* we're supposed to do? The idea is to meet and try to exceed expectations, not just do the bare minimum to get by.

The quest for quality in a mediocre world is not only frustrating but can be treacherous as well. If you find yourself doing more than expected, you may also find your colleagues siding against you. Doing a quality job makes other people look insufficient, inefficient, and inadequate. But the focus of our efforts should not be to please the principal, promote our school's image, or put others at ease with their ineffectiveness. If we focus instead on pleasing God and protecting *His* reputation, we can be confident we're meeting the standards that matter.

FINAL THOUGHT: What can you change today to ensure you are teaching to the maximum and not the minimum?

Lord, pleasing You is the main thing. Help me to keep the main thing the main thing.

DAY 22

We must pursue what   another.

PEACEKEEPING FORCES

Promoting peace in the classroom is a big part of our jobs as teachers. For some of us it is the greatest struggle day to day. We know that without peace, real learning can't occur. But we know that peace doesn't create itself—it must be coaxed into existence. Unfortunately, what seems to happen is that we try to coerce it with discipline, like a shoehorn forcing a foot into a shoe that doesn't quite fit. The result? Feet that hurt.

Keeping certain unruly youngsters in line often makes us feel like prison guards or troops in a hostile foreign country. We find ourselves standing guard with our weapons drawn and maintaining a safe distance between us and them. But there's a big difference between staving off chaos and promoting peace. Keeping the peace is a defensive posture. Promoting peace is an offensive action. We need to be on the offense, not the defense, proactive and intentional in our promotion of peace. We do it not for our own sakes but for the good of others.

How can we promote peace in our classrooms? Each action should intend to build up our students, not tear them down. Our words should encourage, never discourage. Our teaching methods should support their learning styles, not undermine them. We should turn the spotlight of attention to their accomplishments and not their failures. And when they struggle, we help them; we don't just watch them flounder. As you consider the atmosphere in your classroom, what seems to thwart your promotion of peace? Could it be you? What could you change to become a more effective peacemaker in the classroom?

FINAL THOUGHT: Peace cannot be force-fed; its sweet aroma must first make students salivate.

Lord, You are the Prince of Peace! By Your example I can know what it takes to bring peace.

*Be silent before the LORD and wait expectantly for Him;
do not be agitated by one who prospers in his way,
by the man who carries out evil plans.*

PSALM 37:7

BITE YOUR TONGUE!

You know the type. He gains the graces of those in charge by manipulating circumstances, exaggerating his successes, or putting down others. Somehow they don't see through him. Somehow he always comes out on top. In the meantime you go about your days doing what's right yet going unnoticed or, even worse, being trampled underfoot like clover in the summer grass. You're just part of the landscape.

It's tempting to open your mouth and speak as a light shining in the darkness. You want to reveal the hidden deeds of those who seem to prosper at your expense or the expense of others. Instead, you find yourself biting your tongue at every turn. You bite it so much it begins to bleed. Is there a limit to your patience before the Lord? Can you remain silent without hurting yourself?

The answer depends upon what you hear in the silence. The goal should be to keep silent without anxiety—to wait on the Lord expectantly. Can you separate your emotions enough to discern whether He wants you to remain silent or speak up? If your heart pounds with anxiety or frustration from being wronged, it's not the time to make the decision. If you're whispering under your breath how you think God should handle this person, remain silent for the time being.

Those who hide their true motives are not invisible before God. He sees. He hears. He knows. You can rest in that. Don't worry—He'll take care of it.

FINAL THOUGHT: If you bring truth to the table, do it with love, and leave out the side dish of vengeance.

Lord God, You know the motives of every heart. You alone judge. Show me when to close my mouth so others can hear Your voice. Instruct me when to speak up with love.

My enemies are vigorous and powerful;
many hate me for no reason.
Those who repay evil for good
attack me for pursuing good.

PSALM 38:19–20

CAUTIONARY TALES

Those who go into teaching enter at their own risk. There are signs posted all along the way: No appreciation! Low pay! Unruly students! Demanding parents! Apathetic colleagues! Ineffective administrators! Poor public perception!

Turn back now!

Despite the clear drawbacks, we continued on our quests to become teachers. (Were we foolhardy or brave? Both?) We wanted to help shape students' lives. Yet once we reached our goals, a whole new host of persecution began to chase us. Tyrannical taxpayers and pompous public servants nipped at our heels with their accusations and forecasts of gloom and doom. "It's hopeless!" they say. *Why bother?* we wonder.

Our colleagues, committed to self-preservation, hold up their own caution signs. Document everything! Don't get too close! Don't make waves! Avoid confrontation! Don't come in early! Don't stay late! Save yourself!

Do we walk like lambs to the slaughter? Unaware and set up for sacrifice? We can choose, instead, to enter the fiery furnace, eyes wide open like Shadrach, Meshach, and Abednego who walked boldly, trusting God to protect and defend them (see Daniel 3). The path to righteousness is not without dangers or pitfalls, but it is the one that ultimately leads to peace.

FINAL THOUGHT: Has God called you to this profession, this school, these children? If so, don't let others dissuade you from your call.

Lord, I realize that answering Your call has a cost. Though I count the cost, let me not be discouraged from following the path You have set before me.

If I live at the eastern horizon
[or] settle at the western limits,
even there Your hand will lead me;
Your right hand will hold on to me.

PSALM 139:9–10

LOCATION, LOCATION, LOCATION

Sometimes the issue of where we teach seems to be more important than what we teach or how we teach. Upon graduation we're encouraged to secure a job at a particular school or avoid an undesirable part of town. Sometimes we follow the technology trail, believing that cutting-edge equipment equals cutting-edge teaching. Other times it's the issue of worldview that influences us. Christians are encouraged to teach at Christian schools instead of public schools. If we're conservative, we'd better avoid big cities where the liberals live. We're looking for the "location" that will ensure us the best success with students. We're seeking the place where we'll feel comfortable while we teach—as if this were really all about us.

Even if you find yourself working somewhere that wouldn't make your top-ten list of teaching jobs, could it be you are exactly where God wants you to be? You cannot teach where He isn't. No school, whether it's out in the middle of nowhere, crammed between skyscrapers, targeted by gang violence, or where you find yourself the only remnant, is outside of God's reach. He is in the thick of it with you.

Does this mean we don't try to improve the school in which we find ourselves teaching? Of course not. Every school, regardless of its location, could benefit from better curb appeal. We can be good stewards of what God has given us. Take care of our classrooms. Improve our schools. Tend to the students in our charge. Do what we are called to do, and God will do the rest.

FINAL THOUGHT: Whether we teach downtown, on the other side of the tracks, or overseas, we can make the best of any location.

Lord, help me to remember that wherever I teach, You are with me.

Day 26

But I have this against you; you have abandoned the love [you had] at first. Remember then how far you have fallen; repent, and do the works you did at first.

REVELATION 2:4–5

TO BEGIN AGAIN

We start out like gangbusters. We're full of enthusiasm and ready to conquer the world. We work hard every day planning the best learning experience for our students. We expect quality work. We easily point out poor teachers and vow never to be like them. Yet over time the enthusiasm wanes and we begin, little by little, to compromise. We put out less effort, we tolerate more of the unacceptable, and we expect little from others. We become what we hate.

What makes today different from yesterday? Yesterday we planned for the year; today we plan for the moment. Yesterday we read our students' histories; today we'd rather not know. Yesterday we initiated contact with parents on a regular basis; today we avoid parents at all cost. Yesterday we made classroom rules and enforced them; today we turn a blind eye and deaf ear to disruption and disrespect. Yesterday our enthusiasm was something to be imitated; today our apathy threatens to destroy our very testimony.

But we can choose to begin again.

You may not be able in your own strength to recapture the fervor you felt in the beginning, but you can renew your efforts in that direction. What did you do in those early years that you can do again now? What habits, expectations, and values have you let fall by the wayside that you can revisit and reclaim for yourself and your students?

FINAL THOUGHT: In order to begin again, we must become like a little child—all giggly and excited over the simplest things.

Lord, renew me from the inside out, and give me back my first love. You are the source of all that excites me and motivates my spirit.

*I believed, even when I said,
"I am severely afflicted."*

PSALM 116:10

FAITH SHAKERS

Teachers need an abundance of patience to do their jobs. Patience with students. Patience with parents. Patience with colleagues and administrators. And patience with a system that never seems to change fast enough in response to the needs of students.

When there's a student whose antics disrupt your class day after day and you enforce the rules while encouraging that youngster to participate more appropriately—that's patience. When as head of your department you have to remind one of your teachers every week to turn in the reports she is accountable for and you do it with both expectancy and encouragement—that's patience. When a parent calls you two or three times a week (around 10 p.m. at your home) with concern over his child's performance and you put his mind at ease—every time—that's patience.

Your colleagues say, "You have the patience of Job!"

Personally, I'd rather have his faith.

The testing of Job wasn't so much about patience as it was about faith. When things go wrong and you feel stripped of all you hold dear, are you tempted to curse God and turn away from your faith? There are times when no matter what you do, nothing turns out right and you consider walking away. Our jobs as educators require our patience with the continual sacrifice of time, control, and ideals. That's where faith makes the difference.

"Faith is the reality of what is hoped for, the proof of what is not seen" (Hebrews 11:1). We may not see the fruit of our labor for years to come. We may never gain a glimpse of the impact our love, our encouragement, and our patience had on a child. Yet we can hold on to the faith that says, "I, the Lord your God, am in control." What a relief!

FINAL THOUGHT: Faith, like patience, is only truly revealed when it is tested.

Lord, my faith and my patience are being tested! I know that is something to be thankful for. Thank You for doing what it takes to build my patience and perfect me in my faith.

Be careful not to practice your righteousness in front of people, to be seen by them. Otherwise, you will have no reward from your Father in heaven.

MATTHEW 6:1

THE PUMPKIN PATCH

Ideal conditions for growth vary from plant to plant. But even under adverse conditions, some plants still thrive. We planted a pumpkin patch when the conditions weren't favorable, so I was thrilled when the seeds sprouted and the plants grew large dark green leaves. The leaves began to cascade down over the side of the raised planting bed, and flowers appeared, signaling the beginning of fruit bearing. But each time a small pumpkin emerged from the base of the golden yellow flower, it dropped off onto the ground, in spite of such promising beginnings.

Have you ever struggled with the concept of blooming where you're planted, especially if the soil in which you're planted is acidic, full of weeds, or a dumping ground for everyone else's garbage? We have the choice to wither and die or bloom in defiance. But there's a catch. Can we bloom with all the magnificence of our Creator in a way that doesn't draw the wrong kind of attention? Yes. When we succeed with a child others gave up on or secured parent involvement where none previously existed, we defy logic and confirm Christ. Blooming when the ground is lush and fertile is expected and not worthy of praise. Blooming through the cracks in the sidewalk or along the well-trodden railroad tracks or through the worn-out grout of a brick facade draws the attention of even the most hardened of hearts. A smile creeps to their lips and for a moment they ponder a God who offers them this vision just when they needed it most. You can make them wonder how you manage to stay when so many others leave or how, against all odds, your students succeed when so many others fail.

FINAL THOUGHT: Don't be afraid to bloom gloriously and magnificently, but make sure those who take notice follow your own gaze to the heavens.

Lord, I look up to the heavens and see You there. Let those who look at me only see You!

The kingdom of heaven may be compared to a man who sowed good seed in his field. . . . His enemy came, sowed weeds among the wheat. . . . "Do you want us to go and gather them up?" . . . "No," he said. "When you gather up the weeds, you might also uproot the wheat with them. Let both grow together until the harvest."

MATTHEW 13:24–29

WEED-OUT PROGRAM

There is no such thing as a perfect school. Just as all gardens have some weeds, all schools have their less-qualified students and staff members. One of the most difficult experiences during my educational career was watching a dear friend, enrolled in an engineering program at a prominent university, fight a "weed out" program in which professors did everything they could to dissuade, discourage, and dismiss anyone who didn't meet close-to-perfect standards. They were purists, and they only wanted to work with the very best.

At first glance such a program may seem acceptable or admirable, because as classroom teachers

58

we, too, wrestle with wanting a more perfect class. We survey our class rolls and see that 30 percent of our students have active IEPs, and before we know it, we calculate a class average that will never even approach acceptable, let alone perfect. We look for ways to transfer to a richer school in a better neighborhood with a Christian principal, believing this is our chance at working with the very best.

But we don't know the plans God has for those He loves and calls. The child who is driving you the craziest or the colleague whose worldview makes you sick or the administrator whose ethics are questionable may not turn out to be the weeds you see them as today. God is allowing you all to grow together, and when the harvest comes, He'll take care of any weeds that remain.

FINAL THOUGHT: It's not our job to be Weedwackers—our job is to grow, no matter what surrounds us.

Lord, I know Your pruning is inevitable. Grow me up strong so I may still stand when You thresh the wheat.

Jesus told him, "Foxes have dens and birds of the sky have nests, but the Son of Man has no place to lay His head." Then He said to another, "Follow Me."

LUKE 9:58–59

ODD MAN OUT

Most people who become teachers really liked school. Those of us who enjoy the rhythm of the school day and even the smell of mystery meatloaf wafting from the cafeteria in the early hours of the morning tend to forget that not everyone feels this way and that most other people think us odd. School, for many, was excruciatingly difficult or agonizingly boring. Now as parents, when they walk into a school, they sniff the air like rabbits sensing danger and fight their flight instinct because their children need them to be there.

And they think we're the weird ones!

Often when you follow the call God has placed on your life, those around you don't understand. You don't quite fit anymore. You don't live up to their expectations. They can't hear the directions you hear or see the footprints left for you to follow. Some even shake their heads in dismay, thinking you're making an uninformed decision. They don't understand how you could possibly choose this career willingly.

Yet, you know. You know being a teacher won't be easy and that you might not always "fit." But the path is clearly marked. You're confident of where to go because this is what you were made for. When you feel alone, remember that Jesus blazed the trail that lies just ahead.

FINAL THOUGHT: Today you may feel like you're clumsily following a difficult set of dance steps, but remember you're really following God's exquisite lead.

Lord, even if they gawk at me on the dance floor, they'll certainly admire my Partner.

Day 31

*Whoever tries to make his life secure will lose it,
and whoever loses his life will preserve it.*

Luke 17:33

Lost & Found

Have you ever dug through the Lost & Found at your school? Do you even know where it is? I don't think anyone has ever found what she lost at the Lost & Found. But the concept of such a place intrigues me.

That deep plastic bin in the back of the custodial closet isn't just for things a child has lost; it's for things others have found. Both temporarily reside side by side in a place of safekeeping. But there's a catch. If said items are not claimed by a certain time, they are discarded—with no warning and no apologies.

Losing something is maddening in the first place, but losing it forever, well, can be devastating. Just think about the backpack some third grader lost that his parents paid way too much money for. He should have kept better track of it. He should have had his name on it. He was careless, and now it's lost forever. But there are more precious things that get lost every day. Motivation. Direction. Purpose. We can get so immersed in the details of each day that we lose ourselves altogether.

What is the main rule of the Lost & Found? It has to be *lost* before it can be *found.* God's Lost & Found works the same way. He is waiting to bless us and the work of our hands. But until we surrender ourselves completely to Him, we can't receive those blessings. We have to be willing to lose ourselves— for His sake—before we can be found.

Feeling lost? Or like you've lost some of your fire? Allow Him to find you. Allow Him to restore what you've lost.

FINAL THOUGHT: The best thing to do when you feel lost is to stay put and wait to be found. Don't worry; God always has you on His radar!

Lord, sometimes I feel as if I've lost my way, but then I realize You always know where I am, even if I don't.

For you were called to this, because Christ also suffered for you, leaving you an example, so that you should follow in His steps.

1 PETER 2:21

IN GOOD COMPANY

Can you remember what it felt like the first time you walked into a teachers' lounge? Whether it was with triumph or trepidation, you couldn't ignore the fact that you'd finally arrived—you could now enter the inner sanctum legitimately because you belonged. You just may not have realized in the beginning what you were walking into. It seemed like an exclusive club to which you were finally accepted after all those years in school, trying to catch a glimpse of its insides as you passed the door between classes. You assumed the teaching elite hung out there to ponder the possibilities and spur each other on to excellence.

What you found was quite different.

Sometimes it's a den of complaints. Other times it's full of mockers and scoffers. And once in a while it's a lions' lair waiting to devour fearful newcomers.

Well, maybe it's not as bad as that, but you might want to pay attention to who *doesn't* frequent the lounge. It says a lot.

They say misery loves company. But sharing in misery, grumbling, and complaining only brings you down. The frustrations, disappointments, dangers, and discouragements we face daily as teachers fall under the category of *sufferings*, not misery. Sharing in sufferings is a way of bearing each other's burdens, and it builds you up. What a privilege it is to share in the sufferings of our colleagues, and even more, to share in Christ's sufferings. Remember, you are never alone in suffering. Whatever you suffer, Jesus suffered first; you are in good company!

FINAL THOUGHT: When you retreat in times of suffering, you are never alone—you are right where you belong!

Lord, it feels as if no one understands my suffering. Even my family and friends stand away from me. But You know what it is to suffer. Strengthen me in the truth that all suffering has purpose.

DAY 33

Thanks be to God, who always leads us in triumph in Christ, and manifests through us the sweet aroma of the knowledge of Him in every place.

2 CORINTHIANS 2:14 NASB

FOLLOW YOUR NOSE

The newspaper headline read, "Luring More Men into Teaching." For some reason those words made me squirm in my seat. Is that really what we must do? *Lure* someone into teaching? Why didn't they choose a word like *attract* or *encourage*? Why do they make it seem like we are trying to entice, tempt, ensnare, or seduce people into the classroom? Are we really that desperate?

I guess we are. Especially when many districts are understaffed and even finding long-term substitutes is impossible. But when we use a word like *lure*, it's as if we're trying to convince people to do something wrong. If the call to teach is not clear in a person's mind and heart, no amount of seduction should be used to coerce him. If we trap people into becoming teachers, they'll figure out quickly that whatever assurances were made to them are as empty as campaign promises. Before long they'll turn up their noses at the rotten stench that hangs in the air and realize they've been duped!

There's a better way. People are attracted to what we do by the way we do it. If we do our jobs with enthusiasm and confidence and sometimes actual joy, others will want some of that too. We can choose to carry a demeanor that draws even the most cynical critics into our midst and changes their minds about teaching and school. They may come closer and ask about the hope that is within us. They may wonder if they can do what we do, and maybe they'll even take a first step toward a career in teaching.

FINAL THOUGHT: Does your attitude attract followers into the profession or make people turn tail and run the other way?

Lord, I love what I do! Thank You for calling me to teaching. Make me visible to others You've called so they can see my joy.

Day 34

Your beauty should not consist of outward things [like]
elaborate hairstyles and the wearing of gold ornaments or
fine clothes; instead, [it should consist of]
the hidden person of the heart with the
imperishable quality of a gentle and quiet spirit,
which is very valuable in God's eyes.

1 Peter 3:3–4

What Not to Wear

Do you remember the first time one of your students saw you outside the classroom in the real world? Maybe you were out to dinner with your family. Maybe you were coming out of a movie with your spouse. Maybe you were at the beach, playing miniature golf, or even grocery shopping when suddenly you were face to face with a student. "Wow, Mrs. Smith, it's weird to see you here," she'd say. "Well, teachers have to eat too," you'd say with calm resignation. Seeing you in casual clothes makes some students giggle, others flustered, and still others speechless. They don't know how to act and are unsure of their place.

But there are some teachers who wear their

"casual clothes" to school, blurring the distinction between teacher and student. What we wear to school should be appropriate for the environment. Dress codes exist for those who don't know how to make suitable choices on their own. Even grownups forget who they are sometimes. We're role models, not runway models. We're professionals, not peers.

Although it's important that we don't judge someone by outward appearances, and what matters to God is the hidden person of the heart, we must be mindful of why we wear what we wear. Is it to be hip and trendy? Is it to *not* look like a teacher? Is it to gain the praise of our students? Is it to draw attention to ourselves or to become an invisible part of the scenery? Our attitudes and values can transcend what we wear to work each day, but ask yourself if what you wear helps or hinders your role.

FINAL THOUGHT: As a model to your students, what do your clothes say about what you want them to imitate about you?

Lord, You know what's hidden in my heart, but those around me don't. Reveal to me ways in which I can make sure my outside matches my inside.

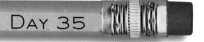
When you pray, don't babble like the idolaters, since they imagine they'll be heard for their many words. Don't be like them, because your Father knows the things you need before you ask Him. Therefore, you should pray like this . . .

MATTHEW 6:7–9

THE HEART OF THE MATTER

Teachers are great at following directions. Step by step we learn how to teach. We follow the models provided to us by a supervising teacher, a colleague, a principal, a workshop leader. The strategies are all based on general guidelines.

- Guideline: establish classroom rules in the very beginning.
- Strategy: have no more than five rules, and post them in plain view the first day of school.
- Guideline: conduct a beginning and ending review for every lesson.
- Strategy: Play Jeopardy with questions from your lesson before giving a test on the material.

Their strategies may not always work for us. At

70

some point we find our own ways of doing things. As long as we understand the *why* of what we're doing, the *how* is not nearly as important. Our strategies are based on our teaching and learning styles, our personalities, and our knowledge base. A teacher who doesn't watch television won't choose to play Jeopardy with her students. A teacher who loves music may help students memorize by coming up with clever little ditties for them to sing. Once we grasp the concepts of teaching and learning, we customize our strategies according to our strengths and our students' needs.

So it is with prayer. Our Lord gave us a model prayer to follow. Some of us follow the prayer to the letter. Others adapt the guidelines behind the prayer to fit their own personalities and preferences. The guideline—be personal with God, yet acknowledge His holiness. The strategy—*heavenly Father, You are the fountain of all holiness!* Step by step, word by word, we can follow His model out of love and not forced compliance.

 FINAL THOUGHT: The example you follow is the example you set.

Lord, I do what I do to serve You and not myself. Let my students see my motivation each and every day.

For I was hungry and you gave Me something to eat;
I was thirsty and you gave Me something to drink;
I was a stranger and you took Me in;
I was naked and you clothed Me;
I was sick and you took care of Me;
I was in prison and you visited Me.

MATTHEW 25:35–36

HEAD COUNTS

What are some of the first things you do when you get your class list every year? First you notice how many are projected to show up the first day. Then you scan for familiar names—either a sibling of a student you've had before or a repeat student. You check to see how many boys and how many girls you have. You count how many students require special services. Finally, you notice the name of a child whose reputation precedes him—it's going to be a bumpy ride!

Then there are the unpredictables: How many parents will get on your nerves? How many students will push you to your limit and end up with detention, suspension, or even expulsion? How many times will you have to check heads for lice? How many students will fail your class? How many won't even show up on a regular basis? How many kids will get separated from you on a field trip—perish the thought!

You have a choice. You can count these as annoyances that threaten to steal your joy and utterly ruin the year, OR you can count them as opportunities to bestow acts of charity and mercy on those in need. Which do you think the Lord intended for you to do? It is not by chance or computer random assignment that you have the students you have this year. It is by divine appointment. And the least of them—the neediest, the most difficult to manage, and the most unlovable—require the most of you.

FINAL THOUGHT: Go and be a blessing, and you will be blessed!

Lord, help me see my students as You see them—worthy of everything I can give them.

73

Restore the joy of Your salvation to me,
and give me a willing spirit.
Then I will teach the rebellious Your ways,
and sinners will return to You.

PSALM 51:12–13

MOPEY MYRTLE

It's easy to get caught up with the complaints of other teachers. You find yourself standing together during hall duty, sitting together during lunch, or traveling together to a workshop; and before you know it, the conversation turns to something that's bothering both of you. A decision was made about your programs without your input. The new administrator made too many changes too quickly. The state's new "all children will achieve" initiative put a stranglehold on your creative curriculum. Basically, you're not getting your way, and it's infuriating.

The conversations may start out with you shaking your head in agreement when another teacher complains. Then you add to the ever-escalating din. Finally, you grumble about your own grievances to anyone who will listen. And then you dread going to work each day.

We all make mistakes. We all make wrong choices—in our attitudes, in our behaviors, with our words. But if our desire is to make a positive impact on others, then we have to begin with ourselves. God can restore the joy of our hearts if we let Him. Call to mind the gift of His salvation; remember the sacrifice Christ made in order to reconcile you to Himself. Then change your complaining ways, and minister to those who also need the joy of Christ. They'll want to know how you can have joy when there once was none. And maybe they'll be reconciled too.

FINAL THOUGHT: You can lead someone to the party, but you can't make them have a good time. Joy begins at home.

Lord, fill my heart and mind with praise and thanksgiving for You!

Refrain from anger and give up rage;
do not be agitated—it can only bring harm.
For evildoers will be destroyed,
but those who put their hope in the LORD
will inherit the land.

PSALM 37:8-9

PLAYING FAVORITES

You notice the little things. The infractions here and there. They're not blatant. A teacher shows up five minutes late to hall duty, and another leaves five minutes early. You cringe when you notice that even though they seem to be slacking off, they're still somehow favored. No one says a word about their misbehavior, and it ignites your sense of injustice.

You point and say, "Look, Lord; see what they do." You know you're blameless in those areas. You show up for duty when you're supposed to. You sign in and out legitimately. You don't take office supplies home. You don't take personal calls while teaching. You do the right thing, yet the hair on the back of your neck stands up, the pit in your stomach grows, and what began as annoyance growls into rage at those who tweak the rules to their own advantage and get away with it.

But are you really blameless? Maybe you don't do those things the others do, but most likely you do other things. They may only do 80 percent of things right, while you do 90 percent, but we're all missing the mark. "For all have sinned and fall short of the glory of God" (Romans 3:23). Any anger or bitterness we hold against the colleague who habitually parks where he's not supposed to, or who doesn't write his lesson plan until after he's taught the lesson, only hurts us. Let it go before it spreads like kudzu and strangles everything in your life.

FINAL THOUGHT: Your sin may not be the same as theirs, but it is sin just the same.

Lord, forgive my unforgiveness. Give me a sweet song to sing instead.

Render service with a good attitude, as to the Lord and not to men, knowing that whatever good each one does, slave or free, he will receive this back from the Lord.

EPHESIANS 6:7–8

TEST PREPARATION

Teachers like their privacy. Even if we have an open-door policy in our school, we'd really prefer it if visitors made an appointment to watch us teach. We are on display at different times and in front of different people. Open House night invites parent scrutiny. Annual evaluations expose us to the principal's analysis. Visiting educators or community members conduct impromptu inspections.

When we know we're watched, we're on our best teaching behavior (and we hope our students will be too). We make sure we have all our materials, the lesson is carefully prepared, and the room is orderly, clean, and inviting. We strive to engage our students, give appropriate amounts of specific praise, and nip discipline problems in the bud. We start and end on time, and during the minutes in-between we teach a thoroughly standards-oriented, interesting, and relevant lesson.

People are on their best behavior when they're watched. No one likes being caught off guard. What we dread is being unaware, unprepared, and knee deep in exposed laziness. It takes a lot of energy to be at your best each and every day, regardless of whether or not someone is watching. We forget that Someone is always watching.

God sees not only the work of our hands but the attitude of our hearts. He knows our strengths and weaknesses and the areas of our lives that need improvement. He is the Great Examiner. If we choose to do all things to please Him, it won't matter who else is watching.

FINAL THOUGHT: Pop quizzes only worry those who walk around unaware and unprepared.

Father God, I know You can see me. Let me always make You proud!

DAY 40

*I pray this: that your love will keep on growing in
knowledge and every kind of discernment, so that you
can determine what really matters and can be pure and
blameless in the day of Christ, filled with the fruit of
righteousness that [comes] through Jesus Christ,
to the glory and praise of God.*

PHILIPPIANS 1:9–11

A PRAYER OF ENCOURAGEMENT

Sometimes it's difficult to know how to handle the different situations we find ourselves in. Each day brings with it trials and challenges, and trouble of some kind always seems to loom on the horizon. Like the Old Testament's David, we sometimes feel surrounded by enemies who seek to discredit or even destroy us. Some of us wrestle daily, looking for one more reason to stay on the job. Others wander the hallways like zombies, present in body but not in spirit.

Friends are happy to speak up about what's best and how to survive. Colleagues tell us to sacrifice others for our own sake. Workshop leaders tell us to sacrifice ourselves for the sake of others. Our own families tell us to get out and into a career where we'll be more appreciated. Where should we turn, and to whom should we listen?

That is the basis for our prayer.

Seek wisdom first. Each day, with its own disappointments and discouragements, provides an opportunity to discern the will of God. Pray that God will increase your power of perception and that you will know which way to turn. Set the desires of your heart on this: whatever I do, may it be to the glory of God. Immediately, every decision you make, every word out of your mouth, and every action you take will align to this standard. And this benchmark will benefit every child in your care. The fruit of your labor will nourish even the least of those you've been called to serve. And this is why you stay.

FINAL THOUGHT: Pray for the courage to do what you've been called to do, and then walk worthy of that call.

Lord, Your standards are the only ones that matter. Help me to focus completely on them.

*"Everything is permissible," but not everything is
helpful. "Everything is permissible," but not
everything builds up. No one should seek his
own [good], but [the good] of the other person.*

1 CORINTHIANS 10:23–24

THE WAY YOU DO THE
THINGS YOU DO

Teaching is as much an art as it is a skill. How we
approach our vocation varies from teacher to teacher
and school to school. We have some freedom to
teach the way we want, but it rarely feels that way.
Everyone wants to tell us how to do our jobs: how to
choose curriculum, how to teach those who want to
learn, and how to reach those who don't or can't. At
the same time there's this need to prove to the world
that we know what we're doing.

It's easy to fall into the depths of frustration,
feeling unappreciated and put upon. But there's another side to this coin. How we do what we do di-
rectly affects how well our students learn. We have
to be willing, for their sakes, to adjust our styles and

strategies to meet their needs. It's ironic that the very reasons we go into teaching become the greatest challenges once we begin. We want to shape and improve the lives of children, but the battle begins when we want to do it our own way.

As you approach the close of the first quarter of the school year, take the time to evaluate what you're doing is working. Honestly assess the connection between how you teach and how well your students are learning. This is a good time to make any necessary adjustments. Your way may be acceptable, but it may not always be the best way. Make the choice that's better for your students, even if it's not your first choice.

FINAL THOUGHT: In a tug of war of the wills, it's better if you just let go of the rope.

Lord, help me to discern whether my way really is the better way. If it isn't, show me what is.

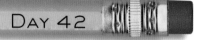

*And who will harm you if you are passionate
for what is good? But even if you should suffer
for righteousness, you are blessed.*

I PETER 3:13–14

THE ETERNAL OPTIMIST

*Do you remember a kind of September when your eyes
were wide and every idea could be tried? Do you remember a kind of September when children made you
smile and you knew them for more than just their files?
Do you remember a kind of September when going to
a meeting meant a time for friendly greeting? Do you
remember that kind of September? Then follow . . .
follow . . . follow.*

Have you ever been teased about your idealism
or enthusiasm by veteran educators? It's surprising
how many teachers try to extinguish the passion
found in beginning teachers. Why is that? Why
does it bother us that others still find pleasure in
their jobs? Why do we feel compelled to educate
them about the reality of their situation—the same
situation we all find ourselves in?

Could you imagine if longtime Christians set out to "enlighten" new believers about following Christ? "Just so you know, once you start to follow Christ, it only leads to suffering," or "I can't tell you how many doors have been slammed in my face when I try to share the gospel," or "Your family and friends may abandon you if you follow Christ. Are you prepared for that kind of isolation and rejection?"

There is something to be said for counting the cost before embarking on a journey, but too much focus on the cost-counting can make you want to cancel your travels altogether. Passion can carry you over the waves of adversity if you choose to ride them out instead of struggling against them. Right now you may be surrounded on all sides by those who are determined to discourage you from doing good where God has placed you. Your current assignment is sure. Hold fast to the buoy of enthusiasm.

FINAL THOUGHT: Don't give anyone the breath to put out your flame.

Lord, I know that even when the waves of adversity threaten to cover me, You are the buoy I cling to.

For it is God who is working in you, [enabling you] both to will and to act for His good purpose.

PHILIPPIANS 2:13

THE GREAT ENABLER

There never seem to be enough people going into teaching. We operate year after year in the red when it comes to personnel. Many new teachers enter without experience and oftentimes without the right education. Maybe you have found yourself in this uncomfortable position—the spirit is willing but the preparation is weak. As teachers we don't want to feel inadequate, unprepared, or ill equipped. Imagine how students feel when they find themselves in this same situation.

Some say our role as teacher is to facilitate. I disagree. Facilitate means to "make easier." What we need to do instead is *enable*. It's not our call to make the curriculum easier for children to learn. It's our call to equip children so they *can* learn. Our heavenly Father does this for each of us every day.

As much as we'd love for Him to just make it

easier for us, God is the Great Enabler who equips us to accomplish His good purposes. What a relief! As you consider your role in the lives of the students placed in your charge, can you see yourself as the enabler you're called to be? What changes must you make in order to equip students to do what they've been called to do at school?

FINAL THOUGHT: God makes us able to do what He has called us to do.

Lord, equip me so I am able to equip those entrusted to me.

Since we also have such a large cloud of witnesses sur-
rounding us, let us lay aside every weight and the sin that
so easily ensnares us, and run with endurance the race
that lies before us, keeping our eyes on Jesus, the source and
perfecter of our faith, who for the joy that lay before Him
endured a cross and despised the shame,
and has sat down at the right hand of God's throne.

HEBREWS 12:1–2

WITNESS STAND

Remember standing on the edge of a pool or the shoreline at the beach with your toes barely touching the water? Remember how you waited to see what the water was like by watching what your friends or family discovered when they ventured in? "Ooh, it's cold!" or "This is as warm as bath water," or "The water's too cloudy. I can't see the bottom." Sometimes you watch how other people play in the water before going in yourself. As a kid if I saw kids teasing other kids in the water, I'd steer clear. If I ever saw someone push someone else in, I'd go back to my lounge chair and read a good book under my blue-and-white striped umbrella. Their foolishness kept me out of the water. It just didn't look fun to me.

As teachers we are surrounded by witnesses—those who wait and watch to see if the water is safe, refreshing, and inviting. They are at the water's edge, watching. Is teaching a profession I should go into? Is this school a safe and supportive environment for my child? Can I trust you? Is God in this place? These are the questions of the witnesses. At some point they will take the stand either for or against us. What will they testify?

There are times when we're tired, ill, angry, frustrated, confused, and sometimes foolish. But we can and must lay aside those things that threaten our testimony in front of these witnesses. Does a child feel safe with you? Can parents trust you with their child? Will a would-be teacher follow your lead? Important questions; and the answers lead to the important final verdict: Because of you, does a child feel safe with God? Can a parent trust Him? Will a would-be teacher follow Him?

Let them know it's safe to go into the water.

FINAL THOUGHT: A cloud of witnesses is a good kind of peer pressure.

God, I want to live my life in such a way that all who know me know I trust You.

"Rejoice with me, because I have found my lost sheep!" I tell you, in the same way, there will be more joy in heaven over one sinner who repents than over 99 righteous people who don't need repentance.

LUKE 15:6–7

ARE YOU LOOKING FOR THE LOST?

Field trips may be fun. They may enhance our curriculum. They may encourage parent involvement. But they also strike one fear into the hearts of most teachers: what happens if we lose a student? Getting separated from the group is never a good thing. And the odds are against us. One teacher for thirty to fifty students is just asking for trouble. That's why we implore the help of parents to chaperone on field trips. The more watchful eyes, the better we see.

It would be so much easier if no one ever got lost. We'd sleep better if no one fell through the cracks. We'd smile more if everyone just stayed on the path marked out for them and never strayed. But we teach because we want to make a difference. It's hard to make a difference where there's no need.

At graduations we especially celebrate for those who struggled more than the rest. We clap our hands together when the light finally goes on and a child finally "gets it." We rejoice at the return of the lonesome dove who wandered away during a trip to the museum. Why? Because they were once lost but now are found.

The distress over the prodigal is easily overcome by the joy at his return. We should never stop looking, never stop expecting, and never give up. God, in His tremendous patience and love, is still looking and still waiting for those who are lost. Aren't you glad He found you?

FINAL THOUGHT: When you teach to reach the lost, you always find more than you bargained for.

Lord, open my eyes so that I can see what others might miss.

Be imitators of me, as I also am of Christ.

1 Corinthians 11:1

Someone to Look Up To

Some of the most practical and relevant measures to come out of recent achievement initiatives are those of rubrics and exemplars. Giving students an opportunity to know exactly what is expected on a given task as well as showing them an example of A-level work enables them to rise to the occasion and model their own work after those standards. Whenever I counsel someone trying to attain one of their goals, I always suggest they find someone who is doing what they want to do *well*, ask them how they do it, and then do it. Simple, right?

The hard part is not finding someone who does what you want to do, but finding someone who does it well. There's no point in modeling your behavior after someone who does a poor job. As teachers we model expectations for our students and give them something to mimic. But who do we look to as exemplars?

Is it the fellow math teacher who seems to produce high-achieving students but does it through his students' fear and trembling? Is it the principal who's got students loving him but teachers hating him? Or is it the department head whose decisions may not always be popular but whose ethical and moral reputation is above reproach? Whom do you follow and why?

Although Christ is our perfect exemplar, we need human examples too. As we strive to align our lives to God's standards, we look for those brothers and sisters whose lives, more often than not, exemplify a faithful Christian life. This is not a life without struggle, without passion, or without mistakes, but one of service, joy, and hope. Find the people who seem to understand this, and consider them your role models.

 FINAL THOUGHT: We are the daily example for our students of the One we follow.

Lord, show me the role models from whom You want me to learn, and let me be an example for students as well as colleagues.

93

*Now we ask you, brothers, to give recognition to those
who labor among you and lead you in the Lord and
admonish you, and to esteem them very highly in love
because of their work. Be at peace among yourselves.*

1 THESSALONIANS 5:12–13

HONOR ROLL

I've had the opportunity to honor other educators
at awards ceremonies. They don't rival Hollywood's
Academy Awards, but they're exciting just the
same. Whether it's public recognition at the Disney
Teacher of the Year Awards or private kudos offered
in the form of a note in a mailbox, we all appreciate it when someone notices we did a good job. We
do what we do, not for the potential glory (which
doesn't often show up anyway), but for the sake of
our students. These gifts we've been given, the skills
and talents bestowed on us, are for the building up
and equipping of others. The *others* are students,
teachers, community members, and even parents.

Everyone seems to have ways to recognize those
who work hard in their communities. At our schools

we honor our volunteers; the local Kiwanis club honors students; our churches honor their pastors. But when one of our own ventures out to do more than is expected of him by volunteering extra hours with students, advising parents, or mentoring new teachers, our feathers can ruffle like a jealous bird of prey.

Can we, for the sake of unity and peace, give applause without resentment to those who sacrifice their time and talent for others? Can we honor them and be inspired by their example of love? When we show appreciation for the labor of others, we show our students how to value the work ethic. Then an amazing thing happens. What we appreciate in someone else, we begin to value. What we value, we aspire to. The declaration of honor is the first step to discipleship.

FINAL THOUGHT: When hard work is not valued, no one ever works hard enough.

God, Your Son went above and beyond the call of duty, and it wasn't appreciated. I'm grateful to be counted among His followers.

LORD, I turn my hope to You.
My God, I trust in You.
Do not let me be disgraced;
do not let my enemies gloat over me.

PSALM 25:1-2

OVERWHELMED AND UNDERPAID

The longer you sit still, the more things will get piled on your plate. If you look like you have time, you will be asked to take on more responsibilities. Maybe at the beginning of the year you vowed not to say yes to a myriad of requests, but as the first quarter comes to a close, it's becoming more and more difficult to justify saying no. Somehow you always end up doing more than you possibly have time for. There always seems to be someone waiting on you to turn something in, show up for something, or call someone. Lesson planning and teaching become secondary to school-improvement initiatives, testing, and secretarial work.

They ask for the impossible within an unreasonable time frame and offer no resources. Sound familiar? Where do you turn in such circumstances?

You can't turn to another teacher. They're in the same sinking boat, bailing water, and trying to row to shore at the same time. You can't turn to your family. They're mystified at your inability to say no and make their own demands on your time. You can't turn to your friends—they just don't get it.

Sometimes God makes it so that the only one we can turn to is Him. He covets our dependence and promises to deliver us from our enemies and their demands. It's not that our administrators and colleagues are our enemies, but we feel the burden of their demands as if they are. We need His wisdom in order to know which demands to accept and which to decline—and the strength to say no when we need to. Can you turn to God today and trust Him to both enable you and protect you as you do all the things you have to do?

FINAL THOUGHT: The answer to being overwhelmed lies in God's promises.

Lord, let Your peace wash over me and cleanse me from the anxiety that covers my life.

97

DAY 49

The intelligent person restrains his words,
and one who keeps a cool head is a man of understanding.
Even a fool is considered wise when he keeps silent,
discerning, when he seals his lips.

PROVERBS 17: 27–28

LOOSE LIPS SINK SHIPS

Have you ever been in the presence of another teacher whose words, if overheard by the wrong people, would at the very least be hurtful or in the worst case, cost him his job? We teachers have a lot to talk about. In fact, we talk all the time. There are students who drive us crazy. There are parents who frustrate us. There are administrators who infuriate us. There's always intrigue in the hallways—did you hear about so-and-so and how they did thus-and-such? We are tempted to gossip, slander, complain, and careen off course with our words whenever we get the chance or find a listening ear. But it can be dangerous to do so.

We may be speaking the truth. We may have a legitimate annoyance or a valid criticism that needs to be verbalized. But those words, the ones that must be said, come with a list of cautions. Pray over them before speaking them. Ask the Spirit to choose your words and guide your tongue. Ask God to make the opportunity to speak clear to you. Never speak out of anger, bitterness, or judgment of another. Choose silence whenever possible.

Discretion not only brings favor from those around you, but it brings blessing from God. He does not value a wagging tongue or a complaining spirit. He offers us, instead, a chance to apply wisdom to each and every situation. Words must not *fall* from our lips like dead petals off a bloom, but be spoken intentionally with the purpose of showing love, revealing truth, and extending encouragement. Our words can be a blessing to others.

FINAL THOUGHT: Our mothers were right—if you can't say something nice, say nothing at all.

Lord, let my words be Your words.

God has put the body together, giving greater honor to
the less honorable, so that there would be no division
in the body, but that the members
would have the same concern for each other.

1 CORINTHIANS 12:24–25

ONE FACULTY UNDER GOD

The sense of belonging is a basic human need. That's no surprise, since it seems we were designed that way. We were created for community. We were created to interact and belong to one another. We were created to reflect the Trinity. We are one body with many parts, all working together. Our schools mirror the same truth. The needs of the many outweigh the needs of the one—and the needs of students outweigh the needs of teachers.

The human body is one unit, although it has many parts. Your school is one unit, although it has many teachers and staff members. It doesn't matter if you teach reading, math, science, social studies, physical education, special education, driver's education, typing, band, art, drama, choir, or technology.

You might be a counselor or an administrator. You might spend your days in a classroom, a portable, or traveling from school to school. But no matter what separates you by department or job description, you are joined together in one faculty.

What is it that unites you? Of course, we know the Holy Spirit unites believers, but in your school that's most likely not the case. The needs of the students in your care are the binding force, and the teachers have been appointed and arranged according to those needs. If you question the value of one teacher in your school as being less important, it's like the eye telling the hand, "I don't need you!" or the head saying to the feet, "I can do this without you." Common sense dictates that the eyes need the hands, and the head needs the feet. Some parts of the body may appear to be weaker, yet they play essential roles. A healthy faculty body requires that each of us respects every other part.

FINAL THOUGHT: Give special honor to teachers who do not naturally attract honor themselves—that way the whole faculty is honored.

Lord, whether You created me to be a hand or a foot, both are necessary to be You to the world.

Let your graciousness be known to everyone.
The Lord is near.

PHILIPPIANS 4:5

THEME SONGS

Our reputations precede us. Sometimes when I see a teacher approaching, I hear what I consider her theme song. The band director proudly marches through the lunchroom to a tune of John Phillips Sousa's. The veteran kindergarten teacher flits and flutters through the teachers' lounge to "You've Got a Friend." Then there's the sixth-grade science teacher who hurries through the hall to the theme of the wicked witch of the west from *The Wizard of Oz*.

What's your theme song? Whatever it is, others dance to it when you're near. It's known to everyone, and it proclaims your reputation just as "Hail to the Chief" does for the president when he walks into a room. Sometimes we try to turn down the volume of our theme songs or walk around with headphones on so no one else can hear. But who we are and who God made us to be in this world shouldn't be muted.

If God has put a song of joy in your heart, let it out. If God has given you a song of grace, play it loud. If God has written a song of peace for you, share it with as many as will listen. If God is your theme-song writer, let the world see and hear that you belong to Him. What do you get out of pumping up the volume? Those within earshot may turn their heads and sing along. Rejoice, pray, and keep your mind on positive attitudes; that will keep inspiring positive theme songs.

FINAL THOUGHT: Drumming fingers and tapping feet always draw attention. Humming turns into singing, and when you sing, others sing along.

Lord, You write the songs. My heart's desire is to play the songs You write.

For our momentary light affliction is producing for us an absolutely incomparable eternal weight of glory. So we do not focus on what is seen, but on what is unseen; for what is seen is temporary, but what is unseen is eternal.

2 CORINTHIANS 4:17–18

JUST OVER THE HORIZON

Sometimes I feel like the Invisible Man (or woman) as a teacher. I go through my day doing what I do, yet go unnoticed. It's as if a disembodied voice and not me, a teacher in the flesh, explains truth and facts to a captive audience. When my words are not heeded or my decisions ignored, I wonder if any of it matters—do I even make a difference anymore? Did I ever make a difference?

Do you wonder if you make a difference? Do you wonder, still, if you'll make a difference tomorrow—or the next day, or the next? Sometimes you wonder why you went into teaching in the first place. The rewards are few and far between. Sometimes you can look back to why you went into teaching in the first place and recapture the purpose and the excitement. But there is also another approach.

Look ahead. When I stand on the beach on the western coast of Florida and look ahead, all I can see is the Gulf. The water seems endless, and I can understand how people once thought the earth is flat. And even though I know Mexico's shore lies just out of sight, it seems out of reach to me. But it's there. It's a fact. Whether I can see it or not.

It's the same with your purpose as a teacher. Whether you can see it or not, you do make a difference in students' lives. God sees the big picture, when all you can see is the sand beneath your feet. Your reward is as sure as Mexico sitting at the west end of the Gulf of Mexico. Sail for the horizon, and you will surely find it.

FINAL THOUGHT: We can't see heaven from where we sit, but we need to live with the promise of its presence. Teach with the assurance that what you do does indeed make a difference.

Lord, I don't know where I'm going! Point out the path for me again so that I may follow Your purpose more closely.

*So we must not get tired of doing good, for we will reap
at the proper time if we don't give up. Therefore, as we
have opportunity, we must work for the good of all,
especially for those who belong to the household of faith.*

GALATIANS 6:9–10

ONE FOOT IN FRONT
OF THE OTHER

Have you ever participated in a Race for the Cure event
or a similar fund-raiser? I have to say I hate running, so
this is not an event in which I choose to participate on
my own. Usually I'm coerced, and as long as they'll let
me walk, I'll go. Certain friends (usually those who love
to run) gently suggest I train for the race. They say it will
improve both my time and my enjoyment of it (what
they're really saying is that it will make it less embar-
rassing and lighten up my attitude a bit). I'm not con-
vinced. After all, I'm not doing it to set a record or get
that runner's high. I'm doing it because it will hopefully
help someone else someday. It doesn't matter if I win, I
just want to finish. The point is just to *do it*.

It's an endurance race, not a power race.

The school year is like that. It's not about how many awards you get or how many A students you produce. And it's definitely not about you. It's about persevering for the sake of students. It's about pushing forward as a child's advocate when no one else cares. It's about finding the time to bestow an encouraging word when you feel like locking the doors and turning off the lights. It's about finding the kernel of talent or ability in a child on whom everyone else has given up. You don't give up. It may not always feel good, and you do find yourself quite weary at times, but it's for the good of so many that you keep putting one foot in front of the other.

I have to admit that at the end of a race I do feel good—exhausted, overheated, dehydrated, and sore, but still good. I ran (walked) the race before me, not for *me*, but for those who can't run on their own.

FINAL THOUGHT: Even if the best you can do is hobble, put one foot in front of the other and walk.

Lord, even when my best walk comes with a limp, You walk with me.

Brothers, I do not consider myself to have taken hold of it. But one thing I do: forgetting what is behind and reaching forward to what is ahead, I pursue as my goal the prize promised by God's heavenly call in Christ Jesus.

PHILIPPIANS 3:13–14

ALREADY CHAMPIONS

When I began my doctoral program, my lead professor began calling me Doctor Caruana. I shooed her away like a fly on a hot summer day. "Not me. I'm not a doctor yet," I reminded her. "But you certainly will be someday, so you might as well start acting like one." Her assurance was contagious! I believed her, and I tried to begin living, thinking, and acting like someone called "Doctor." I know I have a long way to go, but why wait until everything is perfectly in place to start living my dream?

Eternal life is like that. Sometimes we think it doesn't start until we finally get to heaven, when in reality it begins when we surrender to Christ now. So we can live, think, and act like we're eternal. Our goal on earth is the same as it is in heaven—to glorify God and enjoy Him forever!

As teachers we always feel like we're waiting for everything to fall into place, but that just means we'll be forever waiting. We can wait until all our students behave properly, until they all progress successfully, until our facilities are state of the art, until our paychecks rival that of an aerospace engineer, until our budget balloons to more than we could possibly spend in a year. Honestly, how likely is it that all these things will happen anytime soon? The time is ripe right now to live, think, and act like a teacher complete in her calling. Even though we won't fully attain our goals until we reach heaven, we can run the race as if we're already champions.

FINAL THOUGHT: It may sound a little like "fake it until you make it," but if you teach as if everything is as it should be, eventually it will be.

Lord, I continue to pray that Your will be done on earth as it already is in heaven!

Give us today our daily bread.

MATTHEW 6:11

ONE DAY AT A TIME

My grandmother went to the grocery store every day. She bought that day what she needed for that day. She lived as if she were in an earlier time, when there was no refrigeration and people were paid a daily wage. But my grandfather had a successful plumbing business, and they had the latest refrigerator/freezer, so why go to the store every day when you could easily shop for a week's worth of groceries?

It was simple. My grandmother liked going out every day. It gave her something to do and someone to talk to. The grocer knew her on sight. The baker knew her by name. And the butcher knew her by reputation. Daily shopping became her social life. She knew these people as if they were a part of her own family. Relationships wither without frequent contact. Weekly visits just wouldn't do.

Our relationship with God is like that. If He chose to meet all of our needs up front, then we'd have very little reason or desire to seek Him. It's like when we make our supply lists and budgets for the next school year. The supplies come in all at the same time, and we have all we need (supposedly) for the entire school year. Sometimes when we get what we need all at once, it's as if the other person is saying, "Here it is. Now go away kid, ya bother me." But our God is not like that. He wants us to come to Him each and every day, so He can be the One to meet our needs each and every day. And He's the only One who can deliver on that promise. So maybe not all of your supplies came in, or you're missing a day in your paycheck, or that grant you were counting on didn't come through. Good! You're right where God wants you—dependent on Him.

 FINAL THOUGHT: Make your list, and then take your needs to God's storefront every day.

Thank you, God, for providing me with all that I need.

Come and listen, all who fear God,
and I will tell what He has done for me.
I cried out to Him with my mouth,
and praise was on my tongue.

PSALM 66:16–17

HEROES

My cousin is a New York City firefighter. He answered the call with the rest of the guys from his firehouse on 9/11. He ran headlong into the towers to find and save as many as he could from the smoldering buildings. But at one point he could only hear cries for help falling from the sky and didn't hear any from beneath the rubble. Those are the ones that haunt his dreams. To this day he and the rest of the firefighters and police officers are hailed as heroes. They will tell you they were only doing their jobs. And they deeply regret the cries for help they could not answer. The media invited us all to come and see what those brave souls endured. We sang their praises because they put their own lives on the line for the sake of strangers.

Our God not only hears our cries, He answers them. He answered the collective cry of humanity by surrendering His life on the cross. He saved us. Daily we cry out to Him, and daily He seeks to restore us. And yet He receives little praise and rarely makes headline news. It's a good thing that doesn't stop Him from answering our cries.

We can be the heroes in the lives of our students. They cry out every day for help, but some of their cries come as whispers. The ones who run screaming into our arms are easy to save. But there are those whose whimpers are harder to hear. We must make the effort to hear them. We need to sniff around the rubble looking for someone to save. Maybe they'll sing our praises for saving them; maybe they won't. But that shouldn't determine whether we answer their cries. And if someone calls you her hero, remind her you were just doing your job.

FINAL THOUGHT: Ordinary people do extraordinary things every day!

Lord God, You alone save. If You choose to use me as a ladder to a stranded child, so be it.

The LORD's works are great,
studied by all who delight in them.
All that He does is splendid and majestic;
His righteousness endures forever.
He has caused His wonderful works to be remembered.

PSALM 111:2–4

COLLABORATIVE EFFORT

In education we are always looking for a better way to teach and reach students. But some strategies are tried and true; some truths are absolute, no matter what new methodology comes down the pike. The work of some educators is praised in textbooks and training workshops. Bloom, Wong, Gardner, are all remembered for the impact their works and discoveries about how children learn. We study their works and try to incorporate them into our teaching. But even their works won't endure forever and will eventually fall out of favor. One is always trying to trump the other with the latest idea.

Everything God does is worthy of praise. It is always right, and it always works. And since He

Himself is immutable, we can count on His works never changing. The Father, Son, and Holy Spirit work together for Their good purposes and our good. They are not at odds with one another. They are the model of effective teamwork! Can we at least try to mimic their example?

Working together for the good of students should be our hearts' intent. Although our works will never be perfect, they may become the model for another teacher. The free sharing of information should pervade our schools. Find something that works and pass it on! Did you come up with an activity that really made a difference? Offer it for anyone to use. Did you discover a way to streamline your paperwork? Share the secret with your colleagues. Who benefits from your generous spirit? We all do.

FINAL THOUGHT: When students benefit, we all benefit.

Lord, You are the model of collaboration. Train me as Your apprentice.

Listen to Me, all of you, and understand: Nothing that goes into a person from outside can defile him, but the things that come out of a person are what defile him. If anyone has ears to hear, he should listen.

MARK 7:14–16

TURN ME INSIDE OUT

The world is a dangerous place. Schools aren't as safe as they used to be. The rise of school shootings precipitated massive security upgrades all across the country. Security cameras became the proverbial flies on the walls—the walls of the hallways, outside walls, and bathroom walls. Metal detectors became our new front doors and security officers, our new best friends. Fences surrounded our playgrounds, and all outside doors stayed locked. We're doing our best to keep the outside from coming in. Unfortunately, many of those things we fear are already on the inside—and now we've locked them in.

People's hearts are deceitful—who can know them? What's on the inside inevitably comes out in a life. We spend so much time trying to protect our children and trying to protect ourselves from out-side influences, when what should really concern us is what's going on inside our hearts and our students' hearts. We need to worry more about the state of the heart and less about state-of-the-art security.

You may not be able to get to the heart of ev-ery student, but you can certainly examine your own. Ask God to reveal anything in your heart that doesn't honor Him. Ask Him to purge you of at-titudes, beliefs, or intentions that might disable your testimony. Purging isn't always pleasant, but it does clean things out from the inside. Then if the security cameras are on you, there will be nothing ungodly to see.

FINAL THOUGHT: A school is as safe as the people who inhabit it.

Lord, create in me a pure heart. I want my life to look on the outside just the way it looks on the inside.

Everyone must submit to the governing authorities, for there is no authority except from God, and those that exist are instituted by God. So then, the one who resists the authority is opposing God's command, and those who oppose it will bring judgment on themselves.

ROMANS 13:1–2

DRESS-DOWN DAYS

Within a fifty-minute class period the teacher's cell phone rang a minimum of six times. She could at least put it on vibrate! Taking personal calls on company time has never been considered professional behavior, but more and more of us find reasons to bend the rules. Then we get our hackles up if we are reprimanded for our infractions. I admit it's not professional for a department head to dress us down in public, but we're not responsible for his or her behavior—we're only responsible for our own.

"Can you believe he spoke to me that way?"

"She thinks she's suddenly important just because she's become assistant principal."

Comments (or thoughts) like these are evidence

of a hardened heart toward the one in authority over you. Principals, superintendents, department heads, and supervisors are not perfect leaders, but they are the God-appointed leaders in our lives. Just as we are the appointed leaders in the lives of our students and hope they will respond to our expectations with respect and obedience, so are the hopes of those put in charge of us.

Even if you struggle to find sympathy or compassion for an unruly administrator in your midst, consider this—you're called to obey. I can offer you explanations as to why you should obey and how in the long run it's better for you if you do, but this goes beyond explanation. Just as our mothers said, "Because I said so," I offer you the facts—because God said so.

FINAL THOUGHT: If you find yourself ever being dressed down by a superior, carry it off in style—with humility and grace.

Lord, I want only to be clothed in honor for Your glory.

We demolish arguments and every high-minded thing that is raised up against the knowledge of God, taking every thought captive to the obedience of Christ.

2 CORINTHIANS 10:4–5

CAPTIVE AUDIENCE

Although it is true that teachers have legitimate reasons to grumble and complain, there's a point where our concerns become fuel for a lot of negative thoughts. See if any of these sound like they've rolled around in your mind on more than one occasion.

"No one appreciates what I do."

"I'm all alone in this."

"Parents just don't get it."

"Students are apathetic."

They may *sound* true, but the truth is, they're lies. *Many* people don't appreciate you—but some do. You're not *all* alone in this—there are thousands of teachers in the same boat. *Some* parents don't get it, but many do. *A number of students* are apathetic, but many care a great deal. Do you see how the enemy twists and distorts the truth?

If you meditate on these kinds of thoughts, they will control your actions in ways contrary to God's truth and principles. But you can turn this problem around and take these thoughts captive without mercy. Bind them and replace them with godly thinking instead. We're challenged to do this every day at school. Look at it as having plenty of opportunities to practice thinking God's way. Then watch strife, restlessness, discouragement, and disappointment dwindle to more manageable proportions.

FINAL THOUGHT: Common complaints turn into common thoughts that take root and control how you treat others.

Lord, my thoughts betray me! Help me take captive all those thoughts that seek to destroy and not build up.

DAY 61

*There is an occasion for everything,
and a time for every activity under heaven:
a time to give birth and a time to die;
a time to plant and a time to uproot.*

ECCLESIASTES 3:1–2

CHANGE IS IN THE WIND

You have a school calendar, your plan book, the special-education-services calendar, the PTA calendar, the agendas for school-board meetings, department meetings, and district-wide in-service meetings. There's more. Some days you start a new unit, collect final projects from another, generate progress reports, administer state testing, and fill out report-card grades. Oh yes, there's still more. During free moments you call parents, tutor students, plan for the following quarter, hold conferences, take a class to retain your teaching certificate, identify students with special needs, make modifications to your lesson plans, grade papers, and learn the new technology recently installed in your school. I'm sure there's more, but I'm exhausted just listing these.

The school calendar fills with due dates and deadlines, new beginnings and false starts, milestones and progress reports. It's ever changing and not easy to keep up with. We usually meet each new task with enthusiasm and a measure of excitement, but once overwhelmed, we respond with anxiety and fear. The only constant is the fact that things change. Sometimes you begin new projects, use new strategies, or change classrooms, grade levels, and even schools. It's like the screensaver on your computer—always moving, always changing. Try to relax and enjoy the view.

FINAL THOUGHT: Don't let the constantly changing landscape take you by surprise and rob your joy.

Lord, I'm caught up in a whirlwind! Calm the wind and bring me safely back to the ground.

A time to kill and a time to heal;
a time to tear down and a time to build.

ECCLESIASTES 3:3

STARTING OVER

I remember playing kickball on the streets of my neighborhood growing up. There were times when I totally messed up kicking the ball and fell flat on my bottom. My response? "Do over!" My friends were always happy to accommodate me. After all, they'd need a "do over" at some point themselves.

One thing I love about God is that He's always willing to give me a "do over." Every morning, without fail, I can start over. A new day means I have a new chance to do things His way. His grace is new every morning. I have a clean slate; my past sins are hidden from view by Jesus. In my teaching I hope I can offer the same grace to my students. After all, I certainly mess up and have to start over during the school year.

Sometimes you have to scrap everything and move on. Maybe you came up with a project that just didn't work. Maybe your teaching missed the mark, and your students all failed the test. Maybe you went too fast and left some students behind. You need a "do over." Watch out for students who need a new chance too. They may not ask for it, but give them a chance anyway.

There is a time to stick to your guns and a time to give it up and start again. Both have a place in the practices of a good teacher.

FINAL THOUGHT: Is something not working? Stop, then begin again. Starting over is always better than moving forward in failure.

Lord, with You each day is new. I want to show my students what life is like with You.

Day 63

A time to weep and a time to laugh;
a time to mourn and a time to dance.

ECCLESIASTES 3:4

Don't Smile before Christmas

You have to admit—some kids are just funny. The ones who drive you the craziest will coax a smile to escape from your lips. Even if you've kept that smile locked up tight for much of the year, eventually the kids will wear you down and you'll explode with laughter. Wouldn't that be wonderful? Have you ever wondered how much energy you spend keeping a rein on your emotions? They say it takes more muscles to frown than it does to smile. And if I'm going to end up with lines on my face anyway (no matter what cosmetic technology comes along), I'd rather have laugh lines than frown lines.

We teachers think we need to keep our personal feelings separate from how we relate to our students. Some of us follow the adage "Never smile before Christmas." Others are afraid of blurring the line between teacher and friend. Fear that our authority will be compromised drives us to remain as stoic as possible. But I know plenty of teachers who don't mask their emotions but share them freely with students.

For those of you who worry about being too human in front of kids, be encouraged that there is even a time for surprising giggles and stray tears. If the class clown is acting funny, go ahead and laugh once in a while. If the chicks died in the incubator, share your tears with students. And if your track team wins the state championship, do the happy dance! Your humanness makes you more approachable. God made Himself approachable by becoming human in the form of Jesus. It didn't ruin His reputation or lessen His authority; it increased His credibility and His effectiveness.

FINAL THOUGHT: Allow yourself to respond true to your emotions. It promotes community in the classroom and gives rest to your soul.

Lord, let my humanity show just as You did.

Day 64

A time to throw stones and a time to gather stones;
a time to embrace and a time to avoid embracing.

ECCLESIASTES 3:5

ALONG FOR THE RIDE

My husband had a habit of being a little tyrannical when our family took a road trip. He was definitely in charge. We drove the route he outlined in yellow highlighter on the map, stopped when he thought it was time to stop, and went to the sites he wanted to see. Sometimes it felt like it was his trip and we were just along for the ride.

I think students sometimes feel the same way. They're not participants; they're hostages. When we teach, students are a captive audience. They have nowhere else to go; they're stuck right there in their seats. Wouldn't it be nice if we could create an environment conducive to willing participation instead?

Even with all your planning, at times you can allow student interest to drive the curriculum. If you follow the scope and sequence too closely, you'll miss opportunities to let kids get excited about what they're learning and investigate more fully the subject at hand. Some educators believe these detours aren't productive. But every journey benefits from a detour now and then. It adds interest and even drama. Taking time to go more in depth with your students is like stopping to enjoy a scenic overlook during a long, tiresome trip; you need a break from the road. The balance comes in knowing when to explore the side trail and when to keep going. Sometimes you must gather everyone together and get back on track so you can get to your destination. Stay open to the possibilities and relieve yourself from the belief that all will be lost if you don't keep moving.

My husband is learning how to relax more when we travel. And thank goodness, or we wouldn't want to go with him. God is like that. He has an ultimate destination in mind for all of us, but He's not a slave driver. Although at times He has to prod us along, He figures our desires into His plan as well.

FINAL THOUGHT: Plan for students' needs and interests when you plan for the future.

Lord, I know my ultimate destination. I want to take my students along for the ride!

129

A time to search and a time to count as lost;
a time to keep and a time to throw away.

ECCLESIASTES 3:6

LOST CAUSE

I watch a particular medical drama on television every week. My husband likes to remind me that it's not much like real life—real emergency-room workers just don't have nearly that much fun. But there is one aspect he admits is portrayed well—the difficulty in letting a patient "go." We watch as a young doctor tirelessly works the motionless chest of someone in cardiac arrest, determined to massage the heart back to life. My own heart breaks when they are either ordered or gently removed from the scene and forced to call the time of death. Why is it that you have to literally pry their healing hands off the patient? Because giving up on someone isn't a part of their training.

Sometimes it feels as if we are trying to do the impossible as teachers. Teachers, too, are trained to not give up, to do the impossible—make sure every student learns. Some of us face obstacles to that outcome fearlessly and with a confident measure of control, while others see the odds as insurmountable and step quietly away from the table. If doctors did that, they'd be sued for malpractice. Are the lives of our students any less precious than the life of a patient on the operating table?

Do you find yourself feeling as if you're fighting for a lost cause? It can certainly feel that way, but I encourage you to keep fighting. Some would say that Jesus fought a losing battle. Why sacrifice Himself for people who either didn't care or didn't believe and who would continue to sin even after He died a horrible death because of that sin? Because, unlike a doctor, His hands can't be pried away from a heart, no matter how faint the life signs.

FINAL THOUGHT: When failure looms, remember: never give up and never surrender.

Lord, I know there is a time to walk away, but right now is my time to stay and fight for the needs of my students. Enable and empower me to stay when all I want to do is run away.

A time to tear and a time to sew;
a time to be silent and a time to speak.

ECCLESIASTES 3:7

COMING UNDONE

As soon as the words left my mouth, I knew I was in trouble. My frustration had pulled me into a web of compromise, and I was stuck. Why couldn't this child answer me respectfully—for once? Why was my patience so thin this time? Why didn't I notice his mother and the guidance counselor standing in my classroom doorway hearing every word I let loose that day? I called him a name. I asked him to leave. I said I was through. And I couldn't take any of it back.

There is a time to undo what you've done, and a time to redo what you've undone. Sometimes that means you must fix something you've done wrong. If you've been angry and spoken harshly to students or mistreated someone, it's time to recognize your guilt, grieve over it, and show you know you've done wrong. The next step is to restore any broken trust or broken relationship. Education is all about relationship. If you can humble yourself to admit when you're wrong, you will be the teacher your students need.

There will be times to sit in silence and listen, and times when you must speak. Effective communication is the key to healthy relationships. Relationships can cause a great deal of stress, but if you actively look for ways to improve them, you'll find peace.

My hurtful words weren't out of righteous anger, like when Jesus turned over the tables in the makeshift marketplace of the temple. They were out of sin. It took a lot of work on my part to restore those relationships. I'm learning how to be silent.

FINAL THOUGHT: The Word of God says in your anger do not sin, AND be still and know that I am God. Follow both and you will have little regret.

Lord, help me to know when to speak and when to listen. When I can't control myself, put Your mighty hand over my mouth!

133

A time to love and a time to hate;
a time for war and a time for peace.

ECCLESIASTES 3:8

SCANDALOUS GRACE

There are times when injustice calls for difficult actions, and there are times when it requires pulling away.

"How can it be slander if I'm speaking the truth?" she said.

"It could cause him to lose his job and not get another," he said.

"He *should* lose his job, and he *shouldn't* get another!" she said.

"You should be careful with your accusations. You haven't always followed the rules yourself," he said.

"Are you threatening me?" she said.

"I'm just offering you a friendly warning," he said.

But there was nothing *friendly* about this. As justified as she was in her complaint, she finally decided that this was a time to pull back.

There may come a time when you are betrayed by old friends, and you need to break off ties. Maybe a teacher you were quite fond of does something inexcusable and hurtful to a child. If there is unrepentant sin, creating a safe distance is recommended. There may also come a time when what was once done in secret is revealed by the light, and God's judgment drops like a deadly sword. God is in the fight, even when it's clear *you* need to back off.

If you've experienced a time of injustice, either toward you or a student, you may be called upon to stand and fight. Fighting for the rights of children is part of your job. Even during a terrible fight in which God places you, He is in control, and you can have peace, even when no earthly peace is found.

FINAL THOUGHT: There are times to do battle and times to withdraw. Whichever stance God leads you to take, He will fight for you.

Lord, I do battle every day. Surround me with Your angels who I know already battle on my behalf.

Day 68

What does the worker gain from his struggles? I have seen the task that God has given people to keep them occupied. He has made everything appropriate in its time. He has also put eternity in their hearts, but man cannot discover the work God has done from beginning to end.

Ecclesiastes 3:9-11

TOIL AND TROUBLE

I teach would-be teachers in a college setting. I do my very best to prepare them for life in the classroom, but usually they still have to face disillusionment very early in their careers.

"I didn't sign up for this. They didn't teach us about this in college."

"The kids just don't listen. What's the point?"

"I don't get paid near enough to put up with this."

"This just isn't fun anymore."

There are a myriad of reasons why teachers leave the classroom. Beginning teachers aren't the only ones who voice their frustrations this way—veteran teachers express the same things. I think part of the problem lies in our expectations.

We expected to love our jobs every day—well, almost every day. We expected we would influence the lives of our students. We thought we'd be appreciated, at least a little bit. We thought it wouldn't really matter that we didn't get paid very much. We were wrong.

But God never promised our work would be easy. Labor has been a part of God's plan for humanity since the fall of Adam and Eve. Toil is the ultimate burden. Work is supposed to be hard. There is a purpose behind the hard labor, however. It's a constant reminder that the things of earth are not what we long for. It sets our hearts on eternity. It sets our sights on the only One who can give us the desires of our hearts. It's hard for us to see the big picture of how God has woven it all together to prepare us for living with Him in heaven. Yet He has done it!

FINAL THOUGHT: Expect work to be easy and you'll be disappointed every day. Expect work to be hard and you'll be pleasantly surprised when it isn't.

Lord, thank You for this trouble. It makes me long for heaven.

I know that there is nothing better for them than to rejoice and enjoy the good life. It is also the gift of God whenever anyone eats, drinks, and enjoys all his efforts.

ECCLESIASTES 3:12–13

Good Times

Don't you love it when a plan comes together? There's nothing like when you've created a lesson plan, have all the materials you need, deliver instruction, and the students are actually interested in learning it. It doesn't happen every day, that's for sure. But when it does happen, it makes all the nagging voices of frustration finally fall silent.

I believe the majority of us who go into teaching do so because we love kids and desire to make a positive impact on them; we want to do good! We find pleasure in doing good. School years are short, and students come and go quickly. We have little time in which we can make a difference in their lives, so we do whatever we can to stay focused on the task and redeem the time.

As each new school day dawns, we can take advantage of the pleasure God has allowed us to take in doing good. He created that pleasure for our sakes. We can purposely enjoy and rejoice in the good of our labor. It's God's gift to us. When a child smiles or finally grasps a long-studied concept, or when a parent says you made the difference that year, enjoy God in the good. Give Him thanks and serve Him with a joyful heart. Even when the earthly rewards seem few and far between, the good we do and the pleasure we experience are from God's abundance.

FINAL THOUGHT: For God's glory and your good pleasure, you can allow yourself to revel in a job well done.

Lord, everything I do is for Your glory and good pleasure.

I know that all God does will last forever;
there is no adding to it or taking from it.
God works so that people will be in awe of Him.

ECCLESIASTES 3:14

PICTURE PERFECT

As a writer I periodically get publicity photos taken professionally. I go to a well-known photography chain that makes me look so much better than I really am. The finished product is carefully retouched to remove any stray lines on my face, neutralize any discoloration or blemish on my skin, whiten and brighten my teeth and my eyes—they can even make me look skinnier if I want them to. I feel as glamorous as a movie star from the 1940s filmed through cheesecloth. But no matter how good they make me look, I can still see the flaws.

Why is it we keep looking for "perfect"? Perfect doesn't exist here; it only exists in heaven. Our schools are not perfect. Our students aren't perfect. For goodness sake, the world we live in is completely flawed, and yet we question the imperfections all the time.

The only perfect thing is God's design on your life. It may not look perfect, but if you could see it laid out in front of you, from beginning to end, there would be nothing you'd want to add or take away. Nothing is wasted. Even if you find yourself on the verge of quitting and leaving teaching behind, your time was not wasted. When you question why you went into teaching in the first place, the answer comes in God's will. You were and continue to be right where He designed you to be. Why must you experience the weariness and restlessness that come with your call? So you might see His *perfect* will and so you might develop a desire to conform your will to His.

FINAL THOUGHT: Keep waiting for perfect, and all that will show up at your door is disappointment.

Lord, I am right where I belong—right where You put me.

*The Lord God has given me his words of wisdom
so that I may know what I should say to all these weary
ones. Morning by morning he wakens me
and opens my understanding to his will.*

Isaiah 50:4 TLB

Parent Conferences

Parent/teacher conferences may be necessary, but they are rarely something to look forward to. More than once they've been something I've dreaded if I had bad news and I knew it wouldn't go over well. I've been through training for effective communication, sensitivity, and diversity. I've followed the advice of well-meaning colleagues and heeded the warnings of veterans. Many parents seemed to come into the conference either as battle-worn soldiers or cocky cadets. And there were times when I felt as if I were entering battle.

But something changed when I became a parent. My eyes were opened to a new reality. Parents were just as weary as I was. They were just as concerned about what I had to say as I was about what they had to say. I knew what their lives were like, and it made a huge difference in how well we communicated.

The words we speak to those in our charge should not just be facts and figures, but words of wisdom. Our words can give life to those who are weary. Students and their parents need encouragement. They need a word from God on the matter at hand. And in order for us to be able to speak that word, we need to hear it for ourselves. If we're to speak in a way that sustains the weary, we'll do it with advance prayer and sincere thought. We measure our words so that we don't speak callously and cause harm. We balance our good intentions with proper preparation. Conference time can be something we don't dread if we're confident we are speaking the truth in a loving, godly manner.

FINAL THOUGHT: Just like lessons, conferences go well when they are planned.

Lord, my prayer time with You is our conference. Let me approach parents with the same respect.

DAY 72

*We put no stumbling block in anyone's path,
so that our ministry will not be discredited.*

2 CORINTHIANS 6:3 NIV

FOLLOW THE LEADER

Have you ever danced in the conga line at a wedding reception? Someone usually convinces you to get up and follow the line as it weaves in and out of the tables, you with your hands on the hips of the one in front of you and legs kicking every which way. Some of us are pretty apprehensive about joining this line in the first place. We're afraid we'll look silly. But how much worse would we feel if we joined the line and then the leader periodically turned over a chair or two to block the way? What kind of leader puts obstacles in the followers' way?

We are leaders in the lives of the families entrusted to us. For some students we may be the only ones pointing out the path. Our leadership must be intentional, not accidental. We must make a daily choice to lead with truth. If we focus on following the path of truth ourselves, those who follow us will know the way as well. But if we ignore the influence our position holds in the lives of children, we are deceived and may become a stumbling block instead of one of God's lamps.

A lamp sheds light on things very nearby. Our students are following us pretty closely. They can only see what's right in front of them. And right now what's right in front of them is us.

FINAL THOUGHT: As a teacher you are ultimately leading kids to God. If what you do becomes a stumbling block, remove the obstacle or get out of the way.

Lord, let my teaching be a lamp unto the feet of my students and show them the way they should go.

*For everyone to whom much is given,
from him much will be required;
and to whom much has been committed,
of him they will ask the more.*

LUKE 12:48 NKJV

EXPECT THE UNEXPECTED

They say ignorance is bliss. Sometimes I think they're right. Before I knew what God expected of me, I didn't have to worry as much about my decisions and choices. I did the best I could to the best of my ability. But once I claimed Him as Lord and Savior of my life, it changed things. Now when I do what I do, I do it to the best of *His* ability, because mine will never be sufficient. I can never hit the mark on my own. But as much as God enables and equips me, He also expects my best, as does everyone else around me. It feels like a lot of pressure sometimes, and I know I won't be able to please everyone. My principal expects a lot of me. The parents of my students expect even more. I want to do quality work. I desire a good evaluation and the much-needed pat on the back.

The Word of God ensures we're not ignorant about what God requires of us. We should not only thirst after His Word so we might come to know more, but we are to take what He has provided and run with it. Those who know we're Christians will expect certain things from us. If their expectations mirror those from God's truth, we would do well to go above and beyond what they expect so they can see the truth lived out in our lives and give glory to God.

FINAL THOUGHT: When we do what pleases God, we will eventually please man too.

Lord, let my desire to please You always overcome my desire to please myself or others.

*Come to me, all you who are weary and burdened, and
I will give you rest. Take my yoke upon you and learn
from me, for I am gentle and humble in heart,
and you will find rest for your souls.
For my yoke is easy and my burden is light.*

MATTHEW 11:28–30 NIV

A BACKPACK OF BURDENS

Backpacks are common accessories for students now,
but I remember when I got my first one in college. I
was so relieved that I could carry my heavy textbooks
in a pack while I rode my bike across campus. It saved
time too. I could carry the entire day's books at one
time instead of going back and forth to my dorm to
pick up or drop off books as I went through the day
of classes. But what I thought was something to save
me labor ended up costing so much more.

Since I could carry more, I chose to do so. My
shoulder paid the price. To this day I deal with
chronic pain as a result of carrying more books than
I should have. We become so self-sufficient if we're
strong. If people know they can count on us, they do.

"Ask Vicki; she can handle it." They ask; I say yes. At the end of the day I've gotten so used to carrying burdens that I don't know how to put some of them down when they become too much to bear.

At times the burdens we carry are like the piles on our desk. They become heavy and unwieldy and sometimes just too much to bear. I admit many represent simply parts of the job, but so many others represent tasks we choose to pick up and add to our already heavy packs. We need to learn to let go of those. Jesus said we should take His yoke upon us and His burden—for it is light. How can we take His burden if our packs are already full? We need to take the time to unpack our own burdens so we can carry His. His burdens are for the broken people of this world. They are the children in our charge. Maybe it's time to ban backpacks from school.

FINAL THOUGHT: Switch backpacks with God! He didn't pack His as heavily as you packed yours. And He can certainly carry yours if you let Him.

Lord, I welcome the chance to carry You like the donkey carried Jesus into Jerusalem.

The righteous shall flourish like a palm tree,
he shall grow like a cedar in Lebanon.
Those who are planted in the house of the LORD
shall flourish in the courts of our God.
They shall still bear fruit in old age;
they shall be fresh and flourishing,
to declare that the LORD is upright;
He is my rock, and there is no unrighteousness in Him.

PSALM 92:12–13 NKJV

THE VETERAN'S VICTORY

My husband likes to tell the story about a teacher who taught his grandfather and later, his oldest brother. "She must have been more than a hundred years old!" he'd joke. It always amazes me when I meet a teacher who's taught in the classroom for more than fifteen years, let alone thirty or more. Even if her enthusiasm has waned or her countenance mimics that of a battle-worn soldier, the fact that she remained on the job inspires me.

Perseverance has its perks. Just as the craftsman builds up calluses on his hands, the veteran teacher doesn't wince at every little pinch or prick. He works through the pain and does his job even if he bleeds. The work of his hands is praised, not just because he finished it, but because it is a thing of beauty to behold. The more years that go by, the more skill he acquires and the better his work becomes. As a master craftsman, new apprentices come to learn from him by working with him side by side.

We're all in various stages of development as teachers, but there is victory when you reach the "veteran" stage. Victory over inexperience—you've learned what you need to learn. Victory over new legislation, policies, and procedures—there's nothing new under the sun. Victory over disappointment and disillusionment— you know the nature of man and choose to teach your best, regardless. You are a master teacher whose work is known throughout the community. And you are what you are because you followed God and His righteousness before your own desires.

FINAL THOUGHT: Follow the Master Teacher as His apprentice, and you will be found blameless with the work of your hands worthy of praise.

Lord, I long to learn from You. Hopefully, that desire will be reflected in my students.

When [Barnabus] arrived and saw the evidence of the grace of God, he was glad and encouraged them all to remain true to the Lord with all their hearts. He was a good man, full of the Holy Spirit and faith, and a great number of people were brought to the Lord.

ACTS 11:22–24 NIV

CHEERLEADER TRYOUTS

Have you ever coveted the adoration football players seem to receive? Have you ever wondered what it would be like to be carried on the shoulders of adoring fans? I'm not a diehard football fan, but there's something about the game I find inspiring. A single player may make the touchdown, but he does it only after the quarterback throws him a perfect pass, others block the advances of the opposing team, and still others protect him from behind. On the sidelines the cheerleaders lead the crowd to cheer them on. Although most of the glory seems to go to the quarterback, the touchdown is a definite team effort.

Some of us have more success with students than others. Sometimes a child you worked with tirelessly doesn't show improvement until after he leaves you and works with another teacher. On the surface that could be discouraging, but you were a part of that child's success. We can be happy for the Lord's success through another teacher. We can encourage others in their quest to educate and inspire, even if we're on sabbatical.

We educate as a team. We all work together to get students to their graduation day. They are the ones who sprint for the end zone. Some of us protect them from behind, others block oncoming obstacles; some pass them the tools they need to continue, others cheer for them; and still others incite their families and friends to stand on their feet and cheer them into the end zone. We just have to make sure we aren't the ones who put obstacles in their way or try to tackle them to the ground. I think the most effective job is that of cheerleader—we can encourage them to keep running, no matter what stands in their way.

FINAL THOUGHT: Get out your pom-poms. Cheer on the home team!

Lord, let me be the Barnabas in the lives of all the children You've placed in my care.

Unless the Lord had given me help,
I would soon have dwelt in the silence of death.
When I said, "My foot is slipping,"
your love, O Lord, supported me.
When anxiety was great within me,
your consolation brought joy to my soul.

TEACHING WITH A NET

My favorite performers at the circus are the tight-rope walkers and trapeze artists. We watch from the safety of our seats, securely planted on the ground, as these amazing acrobats walk, tumble, ride unicycles, and catch each other as they fly through the air more than one hundred feet above our heads. They know what they're doing. They're carefully trained professionals. As dramatic as their success is in the air, the real drama comes if a foot or hand slips.

It's human nature to be attracted to disaster. Our eyes are drawn to the car wreck on the side of the road. We watch videos showing mishaps of all kinds and are glued to the television when national or international disasters strike. Are we that morbid, or is it something more?

I think we're fascinated because we want to see how people get out of treacherous situations. We want to know that in the end they are safe. I want to share in their triumph. I'm always grateful that the tightrope walker and the trapeze artist have nets—just in case.

And so do we. Daily we walk into trouble; it seems to await us like a hungry lion. We can walk full of anxiety and fear, shaking and shuddering on the tightrope of teaching, or we can walk steadily with confidence, knowing we have a net.

God is right there. He might choose to steady your footing or carry you over the abyss that seems to always wait for you. It doesn't mean the act isn't any less dangerous or ripe for disaster; it just means you can choose to let God keep you balanced on the tightrope and catch you if you fall. I couldn't imagine doing this job without the net of God's love and protection.

FINAL THOUGHT: God's net is more secure than any that man can weave.

Lord, steady my feet as I
carefully walk the thin line of effectiveness.

*Be self-controlled and alert. Your enemy the devil prowls
around like a roaring lion looking for someone to devour.
Resist him, standing firm in the faith,
because you know that your brothers throughout the
world are undergoing the same kind of suffering.*

1 Peter 5:8–9 niv

The Glee Club

Everyone finds a group to belong to at one time or
another. For me, for the longest time, that group was
a choir. In grade school, in high school, in churches, in
communities, I felt more at home in the company of
a hundred voices than I did anywhere else. The wel-
coming sound of altos, sopranos, baritones, and tenors
warming up with their "lee, lee, lee, lee, lee, lee, lees"
enveloped me with such familiarity that I wanted to
open my arms and say, "These are my people!" We could
agonize together over the same complicated piece of
music, be humbled together by a dictator-director, or
sit silently in awe when the sopranos flawlessly carried
the melody at the final rehearsal before a performance.
We enjoyed applause together and endured the critics

together. A good choir has no place for the diva. Even if we used a soloist, we still stood together to support her through the piece.

When you become a teacher, you become part of a global family. Teachers in Singapore struggle with unrealistic class sizes. Teachers in Great Britain are poorly compensated for the work they do. Teachers in China spend more time with their students than they do with their own children. We share in the sacrifices of teachers all over the world, but we also share in their triumphs and their joy.

We are one body. It's easy to get discouraged and feel we are each alone, keeping our difficulties and our joys to ourselves. But that's exactly what the Enemy wants us to do. He wants us to feel alone and vulnerable so he can devour us. Don't let him have that power! Rest in the comfort and protection of your worldwide family.

FINAL THOUGHT: Harmony is achieved by communion, never by solitude.

Lord, thank You for providing me with an earthly faculty family. It's nice to know I belong.

The LORD said to Moses, "I have heard the grumbling of the Israelites. Tell them, 'At twilight you will eat meat, and in the morning you will be filled with bread. Then you will know that I am the LORD your God.'"

EXODUS 16:11–12 NIV

WHEN GOOD IS GOOD ENOUGH

I'm not sure when it starts, but I suspect it starts sometime during our teacher-preparation programs. That tendency to envy, the inkling of jealousy that reveals itself when someone else gets a "better" intern placement than you do, when someone gets a classroom in the main building and not the portable one in which you teach, or when someone gets a 7 percent raise when you could only bargain for 3 percent. Usually we're not quiet about our dissatisfaction with our circumstances.

When we complain in the teachers' lounge, God hears our ingratitude. When we grumble during hall duty with another teacher, God is there and knows our dissatisfaction. And He provides for us anyway.

This job, the one that frustrates you to no end, the one that isn't at all what you expected it to be, and the one with a workload no one else can comprehend is God's provision for you at this time. And it is good.

If you find yourself "wandering in the desert," remember, even then, God provides for you. He gives you the grace each and every morning to sustain you. It is new every day! But just as the Israelites were given manna from heaven during their wandering in the desert and had to gather it for themselves, so you have to gather God's grace each morning. Don't waste any more time being ungrateful when you could have sweet manna to eat, and know it is from God.

FINAL THOUGHT: The promise of new grace every morning is better than good enough—it is God's best to you!

Lord, early in the morning I give you praise. When I rise, I gather up the grace You've provided to get me through this day.

Speak and act as those who are going to be judged by the law that gives freedom, because judgment without mercy will be shown to anyone who has not been merciful. Mercy triumphs over judgment!

JAMES 2:12–13 NIV

JUDGMENT CALLS

When I became a teacher, I knew I'd have to deal with difficult students, but I didn't know I'd have to deal with difficult teachers too. As a result of three years of night school, I had obtained my master's degree and was able to switch from teaching learning-disabled students to teaching gifted sixth-graders at the same school. I was thrilled! But no one else seemed to be.

Before I knew it, I felt like an outsider. After four years I suddenly felt like the new kid on the block again. When our principal asked me to speak at a faculty meeting about how we could all try to meet the needs of our gifted students, it only got worse. Teachers who I thought were my friends said the most inane things. "You probably get to finish the whole newspaper by lunch now, don't ya?" and "You workin' hard, or are you hardly workin'?" I was hurt that they thought so little of what I did for students. They were a merciless bunch, and I hoped they'd never need my help in the future!

One day my former lunch buddy peeked her head in my door. "Got a minute? I have a parent breathing down my neck about how her son is too smart for my math class." Of course I had a minute. I had whatever time she needed. I may have been tempted to refuse her, but since I'd hoped for mercy from others, I knew I needed to extend it too.

People make poor choices all the time. Sometimes they're just plain foolish, but harsh judgment is not the way to go. They will experience natural consequences of their choices, but the life-giving result of your mercy as a teacher or a colleague has more power than any punishment or "consequence."

FINAL THOUGHT: Have mercy, for they know not what they do.

Lord, mercy is given to those who give it. I'm in need of Your mercy each and every day.

"Make level paths for your feet," so that the lame may not be disabled, but rather healed. Make every effort to live in peace with all men and to be holy; without holiness no one will see the Lord. See to it that no one misses the grace of God and that no bitter root grows up to cause trouble and defile many.

HEBREWS 12:13–15 NIV

A THORN IN MY SIDE

For more years than I like to recall, I lived with chronic pain. It was difficult to hide it from everyone at my school, but I did my best to make sure it didn't get in the way of my teaching. I would pace the back of the room during faculty meetings because I couldn't sit for more than fifteen minutes at a time. I would lie on the torn, green vinyl couch in the teachers' lounge when no one was around, even for just five minutes to take the pressure off my back. I didn't want pity, and I didn't want anyone to feel obligated to make concessions for me. But in my quest to appear strong, I never received compassion either.

A similar situation exists for our students with learning, physical, or developmental difficulties. Some disabilities are easy to see when they wheel down the hallway or open their mouth to speak. Others are less visible, and some are even hidden from view. Some students will go to great lengths to go unnoticed, while others have no way to control their explosions onto the scene. They don't want pity, but they desperately need our compassion. Another's infirmity is our chance to bestow that compassion and show kindness.

And in your own painful situation you can do whatever it takes to ensure that holiness, and not your disability, takes center stage. We don't want people to follow our lead to God because they feel sorry for us, but because they are attracted to someone who exhibits holiness even while battling affliction.

FINAL THOUGHT: We're all disabled in some way; offer compassion and accept the same from others.

Lord, our humanity disables us all.
Pour Your mercy and compassion on us.

163

*As you sent me into the world, so I sent them into the
world. And I consecrate myself for them, so that they
also may be consecrated in truth. "I pray not only for
them, but also for those who will believe in me through
their word, so that they may all be one, as you, Father,
are in me and I in you, that they also may be in us, that
the world may believe that you sent me . . . and that
you loved them even as you loved me."*

JOHN 17:18–21, 23 NAB

THE GREAT RIPPLE EFFECT

I strive to connect what my students learn to the
real world. It's all about relevance. What they learn
has to apply to more than just what happens in my
classroom. It has to apply to the world in which they
live, and the worlds they will create for their own
futures. I think about how I've been prepared to
live in this world, and how my job now prepares the
next generation. They, in turn, will prepare the next
and the next and the next. I don't teach for myself;
I teach for the generations after me. I remind myself whenever I can that it's not about us. This is our

students' one shot at a quality education. We already had our turn.

Jesus prayed this to the Father with remarkable intensity. It was one of His great desires to create connections that ultimately connect us to Him. He came to prepare the way for us, just as the way was prepared for Him. We are set apart, and Christ was set apart. Jesus prays for us, and we pray for others. Connections are made for one purpose—to be one with the Father, the Son, and the Holy Spirit, as they are One. It's not for ourselves that we love one another, but so that the world will see love in us and believe in the God who sent us into the world. We are a part of an incredibly big purpose. How humbling it is for each and every one of us.

FINAL THOUGHT: When you connect with your students in relationship, you connect them to God.

Lord, thank You for inviting me to be a link in the chain that leads right back to You.

DAY 83

Hope deferred makes the heart sick,
but a longing fulfilled is a tree of life.

PROVERBS 13:12 NIV

HEART DIS-EASE

Just when you think you know what you're doing, things change. Getting a handle on every policy, procedure, and piece of paperwork is quite a daunting task. I have high hopes that someday I will have it all under control—although if I had my own personal secretary, that hope could become reality sooner rather than later. The workload keeps increasing, the supplies keep dwindling, and the students just keep coming. Discouragement threatens to be a constant companion as we wonder what attracted us to teaching in the first place.

Are you heartsick over lost hopes and dreams of being a great teacher? You wanted to teach. You wanted to shape lives, and you couldn't wait to see if you actually could. But now you rarely see progress. You are afraid some kids aren't going to make it. No matter what you do, someone still fails.

So often we lose hope because our hope was misplaced. We will always be disappointed if we place our hope in ourselves and our own efforts. We have valid reasons to be discouraged; the fact is, life here on earth will always disappoint us. Choose, instead, to place your hope in the One who has already gained victory over your problems with difficult students, parent expectations, frustrating colleagues, and an often disinterested society. Your hope is in Him alone!

FINAL THOUGHT: Hope is faith in things unseen; you will finally see your successes with students when you meet them again in heaven.

Lord, my hope lies solely in my salvation. Everything else leads me to that hope.

After that, he poured water into a basin and began to wash his disciples' feet, drying them with the towel that was wrapped around him. He came to Simon Peter, who said to him, "Lord, are you going to wash my feet?" Jesus replied, "You do not realize now what I am doing, but later you will understand."

MAY I SERVE YOU?

Teaching can be a dirty job, but someone's got to do it. How many other jobs expect you to sift through the hair of elementary children during a lice outbreak? And in how many other jobs would you bend down to tie shoelaces, button up coats, wrap Band-Aids on tiny fingers, or comfort the child who just threw up on your classroom floor? It's not a particularly glamorous job if you think about it. In fact, it can be quite humiliating at times.

We can humbly serve our students, but we can do even more. We can serve one another. I had a principal once who sat by my side as I lay wrenched with pain on the couch in the teachers' lounge. She waited with me until my husband came to take me home, then she taught my classes for the rest of the day. I didn't want her to do that. I couldn't imagine her doing that! After all, she was the principal, and my kids, well, they were difficult. That day Mrs. Baker took my place with twenty challenging learning-disabled seventh graders—a group for which she wasn't trained. I tried to steady myself and rose to my feet to stop her, but she gently sat me back down. "It's why I'm here," she said.

I've carried her attitude of service with me ever since. If there is any way I can ease another teacher's burden or support her in the midst of a trial, I will. It's why I'm here.

FINAL THOUGHT: The needs of children are always in front of us. We have to look a little closer to see the needs of our fellow teachers. Keep your eyes open for a chance to serve.

Lord, show me today another teacher who needs me as the answer to her prayers.

The Word became flesh and dwelt among us.

JOHN 1:14 NKJV

ABOVE AND BEYOND THE CALL OF DUTY

Beginning teachers are so excited to finally have their own students. They've worked so hard to be able to lay claim to their own classrooms. They're motivated and enthusiastic. God bless them! But the real world intrudes quickly within the first year. For many, the biggest disappointment is not the kids or the curriculum or the school itself—it's the faculty. Seasoned teachers ignore them, and veteran teachers discourage them. No one reaches out to them with friendship or assistance. They all seem to close their doors and keep to themselves. It's like when you don't want trick-or-treaters ringing your doorbell on Halloween—you close the door and turn off the lights so they'll think no one is home.

We spend so much time indoctrinating teachers about what it takes to build relationships with students in order to really be effective. We need to talk more about building relationships with one another so the good teachers are enabled and the great teachers stay. We need to step outside of our comfort zone and reach out to those most in need, and beginning teachers certainly fall into that category.

Often we only do what others are willing to do for us first. We don't stick our necks out because nobody did it for us. We don't go beyond the call of duty. We play it safe. What if God had played it safe? What if He hadn't sent His only Son to be born a man? He did more than was expected, yet it was exactly what we needed. Sacrificial love takes on many forms. If we're to be imitators of the Master Teacher, we're going to have to reach out and offer support, friendship, or just a smile to someone who could use it.

FINAL THOUGHT: A closed door reveals a closed heart; open your door to anyone who may enter.

Lord, You said if we knock, the door will be opened. Give me the courage I need to open the door to someone else's knock.

The LORD will fulfill [His purpose] for me.
LORD, Your love is eternal;
do not abandon the work of Your hands.

PSALM 138:8

A WASTE OF TIME?

If you teach older students, no doubt you've been asked this question: "Why do I have to learn this?" There are a lot of things we teach kids that have questionable relevance in the real world. When exactly will I use Celtic history of the early 1100s? Why do I have to learn cursive when we do everything on the computer? Truth be told, teachers wonder those very same things. We work hard on lessons and devote ourselves to making sure kids get what they need, but is it all worth it?

It's a challenge to persevere when you can't see the reason why. We don't understand why we have to go through constant training on new strategies and curricula we know are going to change again within a few years. We don't know why we have to push through the rhetoric of legislators and school-board members who make decisions about our schools without ever talking to us. We can't fathom why we have to keep looking for new ways to meet the needs of a child who may not make it anyway. As much as these things frustrate us or even break our hearts, God expects us to keep moving forward in them.

Any success we have is rooted in the fact that God works through us. His efforts prevail, even if ours don't. He sees our students' lives from beginning to end. He knows where each choice, each action, and each word leads in their lives and ours.

Because I don't understand the reasons for everything, I'm so glad He's the One in charge and not me. I would have given up a long time ago if it were up to me.

FINAL THOUGHT: Nothing is wasted with God. He recycles things and people the rest of us tend to throw away.

Lord, I relinquish the reins once again to Your steady hand. I will hold them tightly with You so we can travel together on this path.

Do not let your hearts be troubled. Trust in God;
trust also in me. In my Father's house are many rooms. . . .
I am going there to prepare a place for you.

John 14:2 NIV

The Portfolio

One of the ways to monitor student progress is to help them create a portfolio of their best work. When the year is over, they and their parents can look through the portfolio at all of his accomplishments and milestones. It can be a powerful tool and a great motivator. The college students I work with also keep portfolios showcasing the tools they use as educators in hopes of impressing a school principal with their best work in the field. Portfolios remind us that even when we fail, we have evidence of when we've succeeded.

I think when I get to heaven, there will be a portfolio sitting on a table in the room Jesus has prepared for me. Inside there will be photos of the children, their parents, and colleagues I helped during my teaching time on earth. And God is the One keeping the portfolio. He's the One choosing the best work and placing it inside. My successes may not always show up when I expect them. I think there will be faces of children whose lives I didn't even realize I touched, but who were affected just the same. I like to think that each time we go the extra mile for someone or extend grace or choose to love or care for someone, no matter how briefly, more photos will be added to our portfolios by our heavenly Father.

When teaching gets tough, just pause for a moment and know that God is building your portfolio and looks forward to going through it with you when you arrive at the place He has prepared.

FINAL THOUGHT: Let your faith be the motivator of great works.

Lord, thank You for reminding me that I am a work in progress, and that in the end we'll both see great growth.

*(They) said to Him, "Do You hear what these [children]
are saying?" "Yes," Jesus told them. "Have you never
read: You have prepared praise from the
mouths of children and nursing infants?"*

MATTHEW 21:16

OUT OF THE MOUTHS OF BABES

Be quiet! It's something we say in one way or another,
over and over again, during the school day. Some of
us are so good at maintaining order that silence rules
our classrooms. Students work quietly, they walk in
an orderly fashion, and rarely, if ever, do they disrupt
the learning process of their classmates. Visitors are
amazed when they walk into our rooms to see kids
working quietly. This is a wonderful accomplishment, but do you ever wonder if you've stifled the
voices that need to be heard?

Some of our students never willingly tell us what
they need. Others can't help themselves. We learn
how to listen to both. The meek fearfully struggle in
weakness and quiet desperation. The wild confront
us daily, hoping to distract us from noticing their

weaknesses. If we are focused on maintaining silence in the classroom instead of paying close attention, they won't get their needs met. Both continue to suffer. We need to learn to read the signs, decode the clues, and quiet our own voices so we can hear and discern our students' needs.

God encourages us to be still so we can hear Him, and so we do. We want our students to be still so they can hear us. But we also need to be still so we can hear them.

FINAL THOUGHT: If you want your students to learn, you have to be smart enough to listen.

Lord, I want to hear You! It's the only way I'll know what my students really need.

Blessed are the poor in spirit,
for theirs is the kingdom of heaven.

MATTHEW 5:3 NIV

DOWN AND OUT

I grew up poor. We didn't always have what we needed. I went to school at times with holes in pants two sizes too small. I learned that I couldn't invite a friend over for dinner because there wouldn't be enough food. I found that babysitting all weekend, every weekend, was the only way to get new school clothes each fall. And I learned what you could buy with food stamps and what you couldn't. Somehow my parents didn't give in to despair. They chose, instead, to give in to hope. And I learned to do the same whenever I felt down and out.

The poor in spirit are those of us who feel crushed by the injustices of this world, by those who do evil, and by afflictions in our bodies or spirits that we suffer. It's so hard to stay positive when you're surrounded by the negative. You're needy and that's a good thing. The opposite is to be proud and arrogant, depending on your own abilities. At this point you discover that no matter what you do, things don't improve. It feels like it's time to give up, when in reality it's time to take refuge under the shelter of God's wings and trust Him with all the things out of your control.

Sometimes you find yourself crushed in spirit because of your own doing. Maybe you made the wrong choice in dealing with a student. Maybe you spoke out of turn and hurt a parent with your words. You've been humbled or even humiliated. This is also a good place to be, because now you can begin to perceive God. He will uproot the causes of your present suffering and sorrow when the "kingdom of heaven" comes into your life!

FINAL THOUGHT: If you're poor in spirit, you're equipped to enrich the spirits of others.

Lord, catch my tears and save them to fill the oceans. If they can do that, then they are worth something.

Blessed are those who mourn, for they will be comforted.

MATTHEW 5:4 NIV

WHEN YOU STAND ALONE

Sometimes our life situations make us feel completely alone. When my mother died, I felt completely alone and felt no one around me could understand the depth of my grief. Great loss tends to throw us into a deep pit. But there are other things besides obvious losses that cause us to mourn and feel alone. Maybe you've just moved to a new city or a new school, and you don't feel connected to your faculty yet. Maybe you made a choice that isn't understood by friends or family, and you stand alone in your convictions. The isolation breaks your heart, but allowing yourself to feel it is what will get you through it.

We don't have to hide our grief from our students or colleagues. We don't have to look for ways to flee from it into self-destructive behavior. God declares that if we're in mourning, we are blessed, because grief can be the path to great joy. Vulnerability creates opportunity—opportunity to surrender ourselves to God and be open to being comforted by Him, and opportunity for others to comfort us. People, especially those who have received it, need a chance to give compassion.

Sometimes it's OK to let your students see that you have a heart that breaks. Not only will it make you more human in their eyes, but it makes it safe for them to be human too. Whether you grieve because of your own sin or because of some catastrophe or injustice, you can rest in the assurance that you will be comforted.

FINAL THOUGHT: When you feel alone, remember that it's the best place to be to receive God's company.

Lord, Your heart breaks every time I sin. You're the only One who can heal a broken heart. Heal mine.

Blessed are the meek, for they will inherit the earth.

MATTHEW 5:5 NIV

MEEK AND MILD

I held my husband's hand as we walked the dark after-midnight streets of downtown Manhattan. We moved quickly and steadily without altering our gaze from straight ahead. The hotel was only one block away, and we were determined to reach it without incident. Thoughts of what could happen to us swirled through my mind. Fear threatened to destroy my resolve, and I squeezed his hand tighter.

And then it happened. From across the street a voice called out, asking for the time. We walked faster. The voice followed us along our path, repeating the question, and then it emerged from the darkness of the alley like a lion bursting upon its prey. "It's 2 a.m., sir. Have a good night," my husband said, just before guiding me through the revolving door of our hotel. The doorman stood between us and our pursuer, and the night ended gently.

We were confronted, and we responded calmly.

We were intimidated, but we responded with patience. We were protected but still aware of the danger. Sometimes our schools feel like the dark after-midnight streets of downtown Manhattan. We don't have to respond with anger or offense when we're challenged, threatened, or unjustly accused. The meek know that even when they feel alone and terrible events seem to call their Lord's power and goodness into question, they can squeeze His hand in the darkness, and He'll never let go.

FINAL THOUGHT: God is good, even if no one else around you is.

Lord, I will be of good courage. I will not be dismayed or discouraged, for I know You walk with me.

Blessed are those
who hunger and thirst for righteousness,
for they will be filled.

MATTHEW 5:6 NIV

HUNGER PAINS

Growing up, I struggled with my brother who is learning disabled. He drove me crazy! When he couldn't get you to understand what he needed, he'd bite you. My mother made it clear to me that because I had "ability," I also had the responsibility to protect my brother when we were away from home. With power comes obligation. It wasn't until I saw the devastating effect the outside world had on my brother that I started to crave justice for him and others like him. He was picked on daily. He struggled with even the simplest learning tasks in the classroom. He had no friends. My sensitivity was heightened to his need and the needs of those who struggled just like he did. I became a teacher because I loved learning. I became a learning-disabilities teacher because of my brother.

When we begin to notice the injustices others suffer, it should move us to work to help bring the world, and ourselves, into a better state. We're hungry for righteousness; we thirst for justice. It should hurt to see others in pain. We're all just one step away from being the "stepped on" in this world. In one way or another we all fall short. We don't quite measure up. We're each alone. And the God of all righteousness hears our outcries for justice. He will deliver us from evil. He will judge the nations. Keep crying to Him, knowing He's on His throne and in control. And keep doing what you can to right the scales of justice.

FINAL THOUGHT: Pay attention to those hunger pains, and feed that sense of righteousness. If you wait until you're past the point of hunger, you'll end up numb to the needs of others.

Open my eyes to injustice in the world, and show me what I can do about it.

Blessed are the merciful, for they will be shown mercy.

MATTHEW 5:7 NIV

JUST REWARDS

I struggle with knowing the line between being merciful and being a pushover. At the beginning of every new school year, I'm determined to hold my students accountable for their behavior and their learning. I believe it's their responsibility, not mine. I set the rules, and I intend to stick to them. It all looks good on paper. But then, little by little, their individual needs creep onto the scene and threaten my control.

One student needs a modification to the curriculum or how I present it or how she's evaluated. Another has parents in the middle of a divorce, has illness in the family, or just found out the family's moving out of state, and he needs a little more hand holding. Another student lives in an impoverished neighborhood, shares a room with four siblings, hears gunfire every night on her street, and is too tired to learn every day. The list goes on and on, and my list goes out the window.

To be merciful is to do merciful deeds and extend forgiveness. We intend to do things the "right" way, but often our objectives don't match the needs of the individuals in our classes. We can't control the circumstances of our students, but we can soften the blows life throws at them. Give what you can to your students. Aid them as generously as you want God to aid you. We can make accommodations for them, just as God makes accommodations for us. After all, He realized the only way to reach us was to become like us. Jesus is the ultimate accommodation!

FINAL THOUGHT: If being merciful makes you a pushover, let it be.

Lord, push me to see things Your way. I don't mind being pushed around by You.

Day 94

Blessed are the pure in heart, for they will see God.

MATTHEW 5:8 NIV

HALFWAY IS NOT GOOD ENOUGH

We often complain that our students are not interested in giving us their best efforts. Some only pass by the skin of their teeth and seem satisfied with that. They're hard for us to motivate. Others resign themselves to mediocrity because they don't know any other way. Some students know what they need to do, yet choose not to. But students aren't the only ones settling for less than best. Teachers don't always strive for excellence either. We cite too much paperwork, state-testing preparation, minimal funding, and apathetic students as the reasons we don't reach the goals we intended to.

The disposition toward mediocrity is a learned one. We learn it along the way from parents, teachers, grocery clerks, bank tellers, and others we encounter throughout our lives. The good news is that we can learn to pursue excellence instead. We do our best work when we're not worried about covering our own behinds. Motivation to excel is only pure if it's not tainted by our own comfort and security worries. But sadly, we often don't stick our necks out for students because we don't want to end up on the chopping block. We don't question detrimental policies because we worry we'll lose our jobs. We teach just well enough to keep the principal off our backs, but not well enough to meet the needs of a struggling student. To go beyond mediocrity, we have to move past protecting our own interests.

Purity of heart means undivided obedience to God. Jesus calls us to aim for the best, not just for "average." He urges us to make a wholehearted effort to attain the righteousness God desires—to do what is right, not for personal gain but for love of God and His purposes for this world. When we choose to follow this call, we will face obstacles that confront us with the question of whether our motives are to serve ourselves or to serve God and others. Whom do you serve?

FINAL THOUGHT: There is nothing satisfying about being mediocre. Answer the call to be pure of heart. Go all the way!

Lord, keep my eyes focused on Your purposes and the needs of others so I can do my best work for You.

*Blessed are the peacemakers,
for they will be called sons of God.*

MATTHEW 5:9 NIV

US AND THEM

We train people early on how to choose sides, and it usually begins in school. We pick teams for classroom games, academic competitions, and every sport. In our desire to help connect kids to a community so they have a sense of belonging, we unintentionally create an "us versus them" mentality. Teachers engage in similar divisive activities. We belong to teams, departments, content areas, and other associative groups that end up being competitive: teachers vs. parents, teachers vs. administrators, content areas vs. specials, regular education vs. special education, elementary vs. secondary, primary vs. intermediate.

Somehow, instead of fostering unity, we create division. And peace can only come with unity. We talk about collaboration, but find ourselves stingy with information, materials, and wisdom. We expect our students to learn how to work cooperatively, but we go at teaching like lone rangers and ride off on our high horses. The way to peace includes people sharing blessings with one another. How can we share from isolation and lines in the sand?

Do you want to be a peacemaker? You'll have to take a risk and disregard the boundaries of teams. Strive for peace, but not according to your own purposes. Promote peace that crosses lines, breaks through boundaries, and brings down walls.

FINAL THOUGHT: The only way to be a peacemaker is to first be in the middle of the fight.

Lord, Your peace came at a high cost. Enable me to pursue peace, whatever it costs me.

Those of us who are strong and able in the faith need to step in and lend a hand to those who falter, and not just do what is most convenient for us. Strength is for service, not status. Each one of us needs to look after the good of the people around us, asking ourselves, "How can I help?"

ROMANS 15:1–2 MSG

THE NEEDS OF THE MANY

"May I meet with you for a few minutes?" she asked me as we stood in the middle of the quad.

"Sure. Let's make an appointment for tomorrow," I said. My family was waiting at home, and I really didn't want to talk at that moment.

"It's about my daughter. I just need your advice," she said.

I stayed and we talked.

The education majors I teach at a local college are on the cusp of their professional careers as teachers. The learning curve is steep. It's going to take some time before they have the confidence they'll need to teach effectively. They are just beginning to develop insights into the inner workings of how kids learn and how teachers can foster learning. They each need a mentor, someone to come alongside and help make sense of this messy thing we call school. Right now that someone is me, and often their needs outweigh my own.

Whether you've been called to minister in a public school or in a Christian school, you will encounter those who need your expertise. We know we're there to teach kids, but we're also there to equip other teachers and encourage parents. We're not all on the same level of maturity. Some are stronger than others. How do we approach those who are younger (or less mature)? It may not always be convenient to step in and lend a helping hand. But watch for people God may be putting in your path. If we're strong in a certain area, we can use that strength in service to others.

FINAL THOUGHT: The needs of the many outweigh the needs of the few— or the one. —SPOCK

Lord, our needs outweighed Yours at the cross. You put us first. Thank You for not walking away when I needed You most.

193

Take note of this: Everyone should be quick to listen, slow to speak and slow to become angry, for man's anger does not bring about the righteous life that God desires.

JAMES 1:19–20 NIV

Do You Hear Yourself?

One of the skills teachers must hone is public speaking. Most of us get very good at speaking in front of groups and eventually find ourselves unable to stick to a time limit less than fifty minutes! After all, we have so much to say, so much to share with a listening audience. Most often it's a group of students, but they're not the only ones who benefit from our wealth of wisdom. Parents listen to us during conferences, and other teachers listen whenever we can get them to stand still long enough.

And then we go overboard.

Some of us like the sound of our own voices so much that we forget how to listen. We think so much of our own ideas that we monopolize conversations. The apostle James advises us to monitor ourselves and become aware of how much we talk and how much we listen. When people talk to us, do we convey that we value their viewpoints? Some of us believe our opinions are the "right" ones. If someone disagrees with us, we erupt in anger because our egos are bruised. We raise our voices as if to say, "Listen to me! What I have to say is more important!"

Students are the ones whose opinions we must listen for. They won't talk if they think we won't listen. In this case their silence does NOT mean agreement; silence means *I'm too intimidated to open my mouth*. Value your students enough to put their need to express their opinions before your own ego.

FINAL THOUGHT: When you listen, don't just open your ears—open your heart.

Lord, I know through prayer You listen to every word I say. Let me be a good listener as well.

*Seek to lead a quiet life, to mind your own business,
and to work with your own hands, as we commanded
you, so that you may walk properly in the presence of
outsiders and not be dependent on anyone.*

I THESSALONIANS 4:11–12

SHOO FLY!

I'm easily sidetracked. Distractions buzz around my
head like unwanted flies at a summer picnic. When
I went to college, I quickly learned that the only way
I'd get any studying done was to basically live at the
library. I'd hide myself away in one of those study
carrels to block out any noise or movement that
might enter my periphery. I recognized that for me
to stay focused and do what I was supposed to do, I
had to concentrate and not allow any stray sights or
sounds into my awareness!

As teachers, distractions threaten to chase away
our desire to teach well. Parents, policies, procedures,
and politics darken our skies like a swarm of locusts.
They easily eat up our time and energy, and shift our
focus from the important to the urgent.

We need to be intentional about filtering out diversions. If we allow ourselves to attend to every little thing that steals our attention, we'll appear as distracted and helpless as one of our ADD students. The difference is that our students can't help getting distracted—we can.

Let others see you quietly and carefully pursue teaching to the best of your ability. We need to remain focused and do what He's called us to do in a way that brings honor to His name.

FINAL THOUGHT: Shoo away the flies of distraction, and do fervently what you've been called to do.

Lord, You've told us what to focus on—the things above—turn my face toward Yours so that I can see what is really important.

A man finds joy in giving an apt reply—
and how good is a timely word!

PROVERBS 15:23 NIV

THE RIGHT ANSWER

Some students' hands fly into the air with the greatest of ease. They know the right answer, and they can't wait to let you and everyone else in the class know it. For others the right answer is nowhere to be found, so they say nothing and hope you won't notice. Both need encouraging words if they are going to succeed.

What will benefit a child who thinks he knows it all? He needs compassion for others. What's the right response to a child who struggles? She needs to learn perseverance. Can you offer the appropriate guidance? We have endless words to speak to students: words that encourage, words that instruct, words that rebuke, and words that challenge. Spoken at the right time, they will benefit both you and your students. But if they're ill-timed, their good intent can backfire.

Consider the child who needs praise, but give it privately. What if you single him out in class and congratulate him on finally passing a test? He wanted and needed your praise. But he didn't need it to be public—so his need wasn't really met. When we strive to know our students, we'll be better able to speak the right words at just the right time. Our words have the power to both encourage and discourage. We must be mindful of their power and seek to use them for good.

FINAL THOUGHT: The right word at the right time can change a life.

Lord, Your Word accomplishes all things for all people. Let my words at least reach the ones You've placed in my care.

*As cold waters to a thirsty soul, so is
good news from a far country.*

PROVERBS 25:25 KJV

PARCHED

Water, water everywhere, but not a drop to drink!
The victims of Hurricane Katrina in Louisiana,
Mississippi, and Alabama found themselves walking
waist high in floodwaters, yet had no potable water to drink. Many died of dehydration and disease.
They waited days for water to be brought in. It was
eventually trucked in from faraway places, but for
many it was too late.

We surround students with "Yes, I Can!" programs, spirit-building activities, and gold-star charts
for behavior, but to some of them it's like being surrounded by water they can't drink. They're so desperate for a word that is meant just for them, one
that shows you understand and really care. Your
"good news" for them is like water to their thirsty
souls. Water is life giving. If it's withheld, we wither
and die. If it surrounds us, but none is available to

quench our thirst, the agony can be excruciating. Good news is equated with water because both sustain the weary. We can find ourselves so wrapped up in our own lives that we fail to reach out with a drink for those in need. Sometimes those needs aren't as obvious as those of hurricane victims or the ill and dying. We need to be alert to those students in our midst who are thirsty, and make sure the water we provide is the kind that gives life.

FINAL THOUGHT: Even though you yourself are waiting for a good word from a far country, make sure you give a good word to whomever is within earshot.

Lord, let me be an encouragement to those most discouraged.

This is what the LORD says: "Stand at the crossroads and look; ask for the ancient paths, ask where the good way is, and walk in it, and you will find rest for your souls. But you said, 'We will not walk in it.'"

JEREMIAH 6:16 NIV

THE WELL-WORN PATH

I've had the opportunity to survey my college students on what their greatest concern is about becoming teachers. They seem to worry about the same things. *What if I can't maintain discipline? How will I keep up with the ever-increasing paperwork? What if my lessons fall flat or the kids don't learn?* These are valid concerns. One thing I suggest is that they try to find a mentor—a teacher who seems to be effective and in whose footsteps they might follow. For some reason this always comes as a revelation to them. They always think they're going to be in this alone.

Relying on the knowledge and experience of those who came before indicates wisdom, not weakness. Too often, teachers keep to themselves and don't reach out for help, even when struggling. They sit in their self-reliance and slowly lose their effectiveness, their enthusiasm, and their empathy for students. They become restless and fitful and lose their way. God told us what we must do to find some rest. Long ago He marked out the path for us to follow. It's the only way to true peace, yet we reject His path and mark out our own instead.

The Israelites walked defiantly their own way. God warned them again and again to turn back and take the way He'd already paved for them. They said, "We will not walk in it." They took the back roads and even the dirt roads. It's easy to get lost on those roads. Why is it so many of us choose our own way? Others have marked the path—we just have to follow it.

FINAL THOUGHT: When you find yourself at a crossroads, ask for directions.

Lord, I realize I've been doing things my way far too long. Forgive my arrogance, and show me the path already marked out for me.

He who loves money shall never have enough. The foolishness of thinking that wealth brings happiness! The more you have, the more you spend, right up to the limits of your income, so what is the advantage of wealth—except perhaps to watch it as it runs through your fingers!

ECCLESIASTES 5:10–11 TLB

BUDGET CRUNCH

It makes national news every year—the budget shortfall in schools. Teachers' unions battle for what the rest of the world sees as a miniscule pay raise, and districts claim poverty while they seek to increase revenue through property-tax increases or bond issues on the ballot. A teacher's budget for the year isn't even the equivalent of the weekly grocery bill of many households. Teachers are disappointed, and many are angry. Some are even incensed and take their complaints to the highest authority—well, not quite the highest.

Do we depend on the money the government gives us in order to teach well? It seems so. But teacher effectiveness is not tied to money. Our provision does not depend on whether or not the bond issue passed. God is our provision—in all things.

We can't serve two masters, God and money. When we agonize over how small the budget is again this year or are crushed by a lack of salary increase, it can lead us to an inappropriate love of money. Its provision becomes where we put our trust. Can we, instead, trust the God of the universe to sustain us?

People will disappoint us. Voters won't vote our way. The lottery fund will not get us out of debt. Putting our trust in people and systems to provide for our needs rarely brings us peace. Even if you teach with a meager budget, God will enable you to meet the needs of your students. And if funds suddenly become available, it's not because of a voter turnaround or district frugality—God gave the increase.

FINAL THOUGHT: You're on the receiving end of God's riches—and they are budgetless!

Awesome Creator, thank You for providing for me out of your riches.

*The steps of a good man are ordered by the LORD,
and He delights in his way.*

PSALM 37:23 NKJV

TEACHING THROUGH TRAGEDY

Teachers were teaching when John F. Kennedy was assassinated. Teachers were teaching when riots exploded on college campuses across the country in the late 1960s. Teachers were teaching when the space shuttle exploded with one of their own onboard. Teachers were teaching on 9/11. Whether it's a national tragedy or a personal devastation, class is in session. And I wonder, *How do they go on? How do they keep teaching?* Is it personal resiliency or is it something more?

Your own fortitude can only hold you up so long. Inevitably it will fail, and you will flounder. Maybe your life is pulling apart at the seams like a weatherworn coat two sizes too small. Maybe a student in your class or school died, or maybe you've lost someone very close to you. How do you go on? How do you keep teaching?

Psalm 37 tells us about a "good man"—one who follows God, trusts Him, and tries to do His will. This is a person who can rely on God to get him through a tragedy. God watches over those who follow Him. He makes firm every step we take. There will be times we stumble, but not fall. If we fall, we will not be utterly cast down. If we tumble into a horrible pit, God will set our feet upon a rock (see Psalm 40:2). When we are doing our best to follow His ways, we can count on His hand to uphold us in tough times—all while the world watches.

FINAL THOUGHT: God is not your crutch, something you may someday do without. He's what sustains your life and gives you breath each and every day. You can't do without Him.

Lord, uphold me with Your mighty hand!

Let love and faithfulness never leave you;
bind them around your neck,
write them on the tablet of your heart.
Then you will win favor and a good name
in the sight of God and man.

PROVERBS 3:3–4 NIV

YOUR ID

Due to security concerns, teachers wear their staff ID cards either clipped to their lapels or hung from a chain around their necks. We have to know on sight if they are who they say they are for the safety of students. But identification cards aren't the only things that define who we are. We wear buttons that say, "Read!" We hang posters on the walls of our classrooms that say, "Give your best, even when you feel your worst." We use coffee mugs that say, "To teach is to touch a life forever." And we sprinkle every lesson and every activity with our love for learning and love for our students.

They know who we are by our love poured out for them.

As important as it is to say words of love or post words of love for our students to see, what matters most is love lived out in how we teach. Are we patient? Are we kind? Or are we easily provoked? Do we keep a record of wrongs? Do we act properly? Do we bear all things, believe all things, hope all things, and endure all things? The definition of love isn't found in the dictionary. It's found in our hearts and lived out in our lives.

When your name is uttered in the hallways and the homes of your students, is the reputation attached to it one of love?

FINAL THOUGHT: Don't wear a fake ID. Make sure the name and photo match the person on the inside.

Lord, let me leave a legacy of love for my students like the one You left for me.

Our mouths were filled with laughter,
our tongues with songs of joy.
Then it was said among the nations,
"The LORD has done great things for them."

PSALM 126:2 NIV

GOD'S FUNNIEST HOME VIDEOS

Have you ever felt as if you were an observer of your own life? You watch as children float in and out of your classroom on their way to adulthood. Sometimes you make a difference in their lives, and sometimes you don't. It seems like the luck of the draw, instead of your expertise, dictates when success shows up in the classroom.

I focused on Joe longer than most of his teachers had. I worked hard to be an active participant in his success, no matter how fleeting success turned out to be. When he left my eighth-grade class, I wasn't sure if he'd live through high school, let alone graduate. The next time I saw him, I had to laugh out loud at how God worked it all out.

He drove me crazy, this Joe. He spent more time

working on defunct motors than showing up to school. And when he did come, his coveralls were covered with grease. So I guess I shouldn't have been surprised the day I pulled into a gas station, miles from home, to be met with the brilliant blue eyes of Joe. No, he didn't graduate high school, but I was happy to know he was alive! He dropped out, later got his G.E.D. and went to automotive school. He was well known in his town as an expert mechanic who was honest (a hard-to-find combination). God watched out for him even after he left my classroom. And I had to laugh—again. God knew what Joe needed long before I met him. He prepared work for his hands and led him along the path. I am forever grateful He was paying attention!

FINAL THOUGHT: God works miracles, even when we're not looking.

Lord, help me to see success the way You do. That way I'll never be disappointed.

Sing a new song to Him;
play skillfully on the strings, with a joyful shout.

PSALM 33:3

SKILLFUL HANDS

Can we do our jobs well *and* with joy? Those of us who strive to improve our skills tend to look pensive and filled with anxiety. New teachers especially have this harried and scattered look about them. But who can blame them? They're trying to teach for the first time and gain the necessary skills to do it well all at the same time. The joy hasn't arrived yet.

The joy comes when our skills are honed to the point of habit—like second nature. I watch as my son strives to learn how to play the guitar. First he must master the basics before moving on to more complicated musical combinations. When he reaches the point that individual fingering and chords are instinctive, only then will he be able to compose an original song and play with the finesse of an accomplished guitarist. Right now his fingers pluck and probe the six strings, but soon he will master the mundane and create with ease.

There is always potential for joy in the journey, but the real joy comes when we can rely on our polished abilities and use them for God's glory. Strive to reach the point in your teaching prowess where you instinctively plan lessons, assess the needs of students, and adjust your instruction when necessary. When you get there, go ahead and let out a well-deserved "Whoo Hoo!"

FINAL THOUGHT: Teaching in "the zone" only comes after continual practice.

Lord, thank You for always allowing me a "do-over" so I can practice what You want me to learn.

His master said to him, "Well done, good and faithful slave! You were faithful over a few things; I will put you in charge of many things. Share your master's joy!"

MATTHEW 25:21

THE PREREQUISITES

As I went through the course catalog with our oldest son, all the classes looked as scrumptious to him as dessert at an all-you-can-eat buffet. He inevitably would choose one and then sink in disappointment when he noticed he needed a prerequisite.

"Why can't I just take the courses I want to take?" he asked.

"Because the college has no proof that you know what you're supposed to know before you begin," I said. "The burden of proof is always on you."

"Maybe I could take a test to show I already know this stuff," he said.

"Maybe you can. But you have to show your competency even in these beginner classes before they'll let you move on," I said.

And he did. He wanted to take second-semester

German (midway through a year-long course) without ever having taken it before. He met with the teacher, she gave him a test, he did well, and she accepted him into her class. I was so happy for him!

Sometimes we expect the rewards that go along with the accomplished practices of a veteran when, in fact, we are only beginners. We'll get where we're going, but first we need to pay our dues and prove our competence. Be faithful in the small things before you can be given responsibility for the big things!

FINAL THOUGHT: First things first—baby steps always come before the fifty-yard dash.

Help me, Lord Jesus, to be diligent in mastering the tasks You've set before me, so that I may receive Your joy and be prepared to do even more for You.

215

See, today I have set before you life and prosperity, death and adversity. . . . Choose life so that you and your descendants may live, love the LORD your God, obey Him, and remain faithful to Him.

DEUTERONOMY 30:15, 19-20

THE CHOICE IS YOURS

Choice is good, right? Yes, but what happens when there appears to be too many choices? In education there is no single correct choice. There are multiple ways to meet the needs of students. Every child is different. Every family is different. Every school is different. "One size fits all" just doesn't work in education. (Come to think of it, that never works, does it?)

Teachers struggle with choices every day. Give no homework and do everything in class, or give homework daily for continual practice? Base your grades on points, percentages, or letter grades? Let questionable student behavior pass or stamp it out right away? Pass a student even if the grades don't support it, or let the natural consequence of not doing the work fall where it may? One way or the other, day by day, we face practical, organizational, personal, professional, and ethical choices. It would be easier if someone would just tell us what to do.

Parents also struggle with the choices presented to them. Public or private school, or perhaps home-school? Charter school or magnet school? Full-day kindergarten or half-day? On and on it goes, where it stops, nobody knows! Wouldn't it be nice if we could just safely send our kids to their neighborhood schools and feel confident that their needs would be met? The choice just isn't that simple anymore.

As complicated as this all seems, our choices are simpler when we reduce them to the basics. God offers us two choices every day—life or death. Choosing life means you follow His will. Choosing death means you follow your own. No matter what other choices we make in this world, this daily decision is fundamental. It is that black-and-white, that cut-and-dried. Which choice will you make today?

FINAL THOUGHT: Find yourself choosing the lesser of two evils? Walk away from both, and choose life instead!

Show me, Lord, on a daily basis what it means to choose life through all the little decisions I must make.

DAY 109

One who isolates himself pursues [selfish] desires;
he rebels against all sound judgment.

PROVERBS 18:1

ALL BY MYSELF

I frequently caution teachers not to spend too much time in the teachers' lounge because of its tendency to foster grumbling, gossip, and discontent. However, choosing to completely isolate oneself has its own consequences.

I wasn't comfortable. I was the "new" teacher and knew no one. I tiptoed into the teachers' lounge for lunch because I'd heard rumors of an incredible chicken Caesar salad I just couldn't resist. I stood there with my tray in hand and scanned the room for an open place at a table. There wasn't one. So I sat on the torn and well-worn green couch near the back wall and balanced my tray on my knees to eat. After fifteen excruciating minutes of a teetering tray and three interruptions from phone calls, I gave up and returned to the sanctuary of my own classroom to finish my lunch in perfect peace (and balance!). I didn't return to eat in the lounge for the rest of the semester. I had no idea my absence was noticed.

It took my next-door teaching neighbor to give me a heads-up. She gently suggested I might join the others at lunchtime so I wouldn't be perceived as elitist or conceited. Me? Conceited? But perception is everything, and everyone had decided I thought I was better than they were—an attitude certainly not conducive to faculty harmony. Then I wondered— *could they be right?*

In a way, they were.

My choice to eat alone was rooted in my sense of discomfort and my own preferences. It had nothing to do with building relationships with my new faculty. It had everything to do with me. I learned the teachers' lounge might not be the best place to be *all* the time, but being perceived as a separatist was worse.

FINAL THOUGHT: If you find yourself alone, usually it's because you chose to be alone.

Lord, You made us for community. Help me get over my discomfort and reach out in friendship to the faculty You chose for me.

DAY 110

Therefore be alert, since you don't know when the master of the house is coming—whether in the evening or at midnight or at the crowing of the rooster or early in the morning. Otherwise, he might come suddenly and find you sleeping. And what I say to you, I say to everyone: Be alert!

MARK 13:35–37

SURPRISE INSPECTIONS

From the very beginning of their careers, teachers are observed and evaluated on their teaching skills. Even education students endure this nerve-wracking experience. It's one thing to be supervised, yet another to be evaluated. Scheduled observations are easier. You have the chance to prepare and make sure your students are on their best behavior. Surprise visits are another story. You're caught off guard, "in the act" of doing what you do. If your room is a mess, they'll notice; if your lesson isn't well prepared, they'll make note of it; if your students are unruly, they'll remember.

Jesus will make a surprise inspection someday. He said so. He didn't tell us the day or time, but we know He's coming. I wonder what He'll find me doing when He shows up. My hope is that He'll find me well prepared and working diligently.

When I make surprise visits to my interns, I don't expect perfection. I hope I will find them working diligently. I hope they will always be prepared. I hope they won't be ruffled by my appearance in their classroom without warning. After all, I told them to expect me—sometime. We have "open door" policies in our schools. Parents and other visitors may come and observe at any time. If it hasn't happened to you yet, it will. So I'll give you the best advice I've got—be alert!

FINAL THOUGHT: You can't "be ready" until you "get ready." Be intentional about being prepared.

Lord, like a thief in the night You will come. I want to be ready!

221

Rejoice in hope; be patient in affliction;
be persistent in prayer.

ROMANS 12:12

STAYING ON TASK

One of the things you learn early on as a teacher is to give clear and specific directions. Otherwise, your students just stare at you, dumbfounded and motionless. Not only do we have to tell them what to do, we have to tell them *how* to do it. Write neatly. Finish the level completely. Do the problems correctly. Speak in turn. Work quietly. We let students know we don't just expect them to do the work, but to do it in a manner worthy of praise—our praise.

Giving specific instructions sets kids up to succeed. They know, if you tell them, how to master the content and can then stay focused on the task. Mr. Donald tells his students exactly what they need to do to get an A in his math class. He never tells them what to do to get a C, a D, or an F. That's not the goal. If they try and fail, he lets them try again, and again, and again. Persistence pays off. Most choose to succeed.

It's a good thing God not only tells us to follow Him, but *how* to follow Him. He commands us to do something, but then tells us how to do it in a way worthy of His praise. How should we respond to suffering and affliction? With patience. How should we pray? With persistence. How should we respond to the gift of each day? With thanksgiving. God is very specific about His goals for us. And if we fail, He'll let us retake the test again, and again, and again until we succeed. How can we learn from the Master Teacher to become better teachers ourselves?

FINAL THOUGHT: Define the expectation, and it's much easier to stay on task.

Lord, let me thirst after Your Word so I might know how You want me to live this life You've given me.

We are fools for Christ, but you are wise in Christ! We are weak, but you are strong! You are distinguished, but we are dishonored! Up to the present hour we are both hungry and thirsty; we are poorly clothed, roughly treated, homeless; we labor, working with our own hands. When we are reviled, we bless; when we are persecuted, we endure it; when we are slandered, we entreat.

1 CORINTHIANS 4:10–13

PAVING THE WAY

Once I had a chance to see how things work behind the scenes of a movie production. There are hundreds of people whose jobs make the actors look good. Their names flash on the screen credits, but you've never heard of them, nor would you ever pay attention to them. They build scenery; transport equipment; drive people around; make sure they're fed; do their hair, makeup, and wardrobe; run errands. There are plumbers, electricians, carpenters, designers, stunt people, and truck drivers. They are not the "beautiful people," and they'll never walk the red carpet. They pave the way so others don't stumble or look foolish.

As teachers we pave the way for both our students and the teachers who will come after us. We do the dirty work. We take the heat. We do what it takes to make their experience as smooth as possible. To many we are invisible, yet society seems to blame us for many of its ills. We experience lack of respect and lack of involvement from parents. We battle the wills of our students, when all we really want to do is help.

Sometimes it seems hopeless, but we do not labor in vain. We can endure the persecution, bless those who curse us, and walk with our heads high when others speak ill of us. Our feet will be steadied on the path, and in doing so we flatten the ground for those who will come after us.

FINAL THOUGHT: Be like a paving stone—someone who lays down his life to make the path smoother for those who come next.

Lord, You paved the way for me. I want to pave the way for those who come after me.

The instruction of the LORD is perfect,
reviving the soul;
the testimony of the LORD is trustworthy,
making the inexperienced wise.

PSALM 19:7

EXPERIENCE TEACHES

They say that you learn by doing. This is quite true, but not always possible. Is learning by experience the only way? We share with students daily lessons that enable them to make wise choices, not via their experiences but through the experiences of others. They learn, for example, that absolute power corrupts absolutely, not because they themselves have had that kind of power, but because they learned about those throughout history who did.

Our advice, our wisdom, when shared with others, adds to their own experience. They discover that people can heal from heartache by hearing how you recovered from yours. They learn that pursuing their dreams is the first step to making them a reality by hearing your story. They know that "this too shall pass" because it passed for you. Our experiences are potent teachers for others when we're willing to share them and they're willing to listen.

Jesus modeled this truth by His life, death, resurrection, and teachings. We don't have to experience crucifixion to know suffering. We don't have to spend forty days in the desert battling wills with the devil in order to understand the challenge of temptation. We don't have to be whipped, stripped, and ridiculed as "The King of the Jews" to know humiliation. His testimony is enough for us to gain wisdom. The fear of the Lord is the beginning of wisdom. We can have a healthy respect for who God is and what He's done for us and, thereby, become wise.

FINAL THOUGHT: Our students will gain wisdom through their own experiences, but they can also gain wisdom by witnessing ours.

Lord, help me be mindful that my students' eyes are always upon me.

Now in a large house there are not only gold and silver bowls, but also those of wood and earthenware, some for special use, some for ordinary. So if anyone purifies himself from these things, he will be a special instrument, set apart, useful to the Master, prepared for every good work.

2 Timothy 2:20–21

Honor Roll

Every grading period, some students strive to make the honor roll, while others could not care less. For some it is a matter of ability; for others it's a matter of drive. But even those whose abilities are limited can esteem themselves by their very persistence. If their efforts don't result in the coveted 3.5 grade-point average, their diligence will still pay off in the end and they will find success. Those who choose not to pursue excellence, even those who have the God-given ability but squander it, will not find their futures bright. They will not be useful or prepared for "every good work."

Students aren't the only ones who should seek

the honor roll. Teachers would do well to strive for a high GPA. There are some who have natural teaching ability and polish that ability for the good of their students. There are others whose teaching might be considered substandard, and yet they refuse to seek out ways to improve. They scoff at those who take professional development seriously and, instead, sit comfortably in complacency. Their work is not useful. They bring dishonor on the profession and contaminate it with their mediocrity. As critical as this may sound, the legislative desire to put a "quality" teacher in every classroom is a good one.

FINAL THOUGHT: Our call is one of honor. Do you seek to make the honor roll this time?

Set me apart, Lord. Teach me to be diligent, prepared, and useful for You.

*Flee from youthful passions, and pursue righteousness,
faith, love, and peace, along with those who call on the
Lord from a pure heart. But reject foolish and ignorant
disputes, knowing that they breed quarrels.*

2 TIMOTHY 2:22–23

A BLAST FROM THE PAST

For some reason many teachers behave in faculty meetings like high-school students in a school assembly. All the guys sit together in the back of the room. They lean their chairs on two legs against the wall and sit with their arms crossed with an "I dare you to tell me something I'll care about" look on their faces. The gals sit in their cliques and whisper to one another while the meeting leader is talking. Then there are those who sit silently as if invisible and whose presence is barely noticed. The rebels, the know-it-alls, the popular ones, the jocks, the nerds, the goody-goodies, and the misfits all walk the halls in grown-up bodies.

We find ourselves falling into the foolish behaviors of "old" that cause division instead of unity. We argue about the most inconsequential things and rival for the spot of top dog whenever possible. We focus on the wrong things. The things of the earth, the status, the positions we seek—are all treasures we hoard, but they will pass away. Can we focus, instead, on the eternal treasures like faith, love, and peace? If you pursue peace, you gain unity. If you find faith, you gain godly perspective. If you love, you save.

The next time you find yourself in a faculty meeting and everyone around you has fallen into their old habits, try to see them as God sees them—people He loves and sent His Son to save. Break out of the mold, and be the one to act like a grownup.

FINAL THOUGHT: You'll have to release the past if you're going to take hold of the future.

Thank you, Father, for loving us even when we are caught up in youthful behaviors and foolish disputes.

The Lord's slave must not quarrel, but must be gentle to everyone, able to teach, and patient, instructing his opponents with gentleness. Perhaps God will grant them repentance to know the truth. Then they may come to their senses and escape the Devil's trap, having been captured by him to do his will.

2 TIMOTHY 2:24–26

HARDHEADED ARGUMENTS

You will never win an argument with some people. The parent who calls you at least once a week criticizing your teaching becomes both discouraging and tiresome. The student who stands defiantly at your desk and says, "I don't have to listen to you. My mom said so," makes it difficult for you to have a comeback. The principal who doesn't see the value in your request for a sink in your art classroom just doesn't get it. It seems you constantly run into people who pose obstacles to your way of thinking. Arguing with them feels like you're banging your head against the wall. It hurts! I strongly suggest you stop.

What should our response be to those who seem to argue for argument's sake or to those who just don't get it? Do we walk away and avoid them? Do we look for creative ways to get our point across in hopes that they'll finally listen? Scripture offers a wildly different perspective: Our goal is not to win the argument. Our goal is to win souls. We can answer with a kind word and a gentle spirit. We can continue to teach with patience. We can hope that one day God will open their eyes to the truth, but we can refuse to let that possibility determine how we interact with them. We can also humbly acknowledge that we may be wrong and ask God to let us see the truth. They might be your opponents, and you play for different sides, but you can rest in the fact that God always wins!

FINAL THOUGHT: Play with the confidence that you're already on the winning team.

Lord, help me to be gentle to everyone, even those with whom I disagree.

Proclaim the message;
persist in it whether convenient or not;
rebuke, correct, and encourage
with great patience and teaching.

2 TIMOTHY 4:2

LIFE ENCOUNTER

Our curricula not withstanding, we have a message to give our students—there is life after school, and it can be an abundant life. There is so much more to what we teach than facts. Our attitudes, our values, and our very lives become fodder for our lessons. It's not always convenient for our lives to be on display, but it's necessary if students are really to discover what's important.

Even when I teach education majors, I know my life is a model they will follow. I have to remind them over and over again to stay focused—it's all about the kids, not us. I have to correct their thinking if it's off-center. I have to encourage them to keep trying when they want to give up. But it's more than "telling" them what to do; I must "show" them how to do it. That takes more time than I seem to have in a day.

But I persist. I continue to offer them my life as a testimony—warts and all. Ours is a holy calling, one that has the power to bring others to Christ. Our teaching can be an evangelistic tool. How we prepare a lesson, how we teach that lesson, and how we respond to our students' understanding (or lack thereof) of that lesson shows our love for them. Even when we discipline or correct them, they can know we love them. We can do this because Jesus laid down His life for us to show His great love.

FINAL THOUGHT: A life displayed is a life examined. What do your students discover when they look at yours?

My God, thank You for leaving me a model to follow. Encourage me to bare who I am to all.

*For the time will come when they will not tolerate
sound doctrine, but according to their own desires, will
accumulate teachers for themselves because they have an
itch to hear something new. They will turn away from
hearing the truth and will turn aside to myths.*

2 Timothy 4:3–4

A Trophy for Everyone

When our boys played soccer, I couldn't wait for
them to experience a taste of competition. Their particular program touted itself as the competitive side
of a strictly recreational sport. Kids had to try out
for a team. The uniforms cost more. They practiced
twice a week. And there were three times as many
games compared to the recreational league.

Unfortunately, I'd misunderstood the goals of
this league—or maybe they were misrepresented.
Even though our team didn't fare well in the
competition, everyone got a trophy! I was sorely
disappointed.

Just two years earlier this league had been the
"competitive" one, but after parents complained that

losing hurt their children's self-esteem and some threatened to quit the league, the management gave in and made sure *everyone* was a winner. The kids didn't have to feel the pain of falling short of a goal nor learn what it means to *earn* a reward. And what did those parents learn? They learned that if they don't like the truth, they can easily find some way to confirm the myths they prefer.

Our schools have done the same thing. Discipline, competition, ability-level grouping, awards, and even honor societies have been replaced with alternative-behavior plans, heterogeneous grouping, participation awards, and "My child showed up at Smith Middle School!" bumper stickers. I can't fight the entire system, but I'm always trying to steer things back in the direction of "sound doctrine." We all need to be wary of myths and fads masquerading as truth.

FINAL THOUGHT: If someone has an itch in his ear, he can't hear anything you have to say.

Show me what's real, God. Let me not reject sound doctrine, but let me embrace what's right, no matter what everyone else is doing.

*But as for you, keep a clear head about everything,
endure hardship, do the work of an evangelist,
fulfill your ministry.*

2 Timothy 4:5

Why Stay?

Teachers often find themselves in the position of defending themselves. They defend their choice to teach in the first place to friends, family, and even other teachers. They defend their public- vs. private-school choice to well-meaning fellow Christians. They defend their choice to stay, even when everyone else in society tells them they should quit.

"I could never do what you do," someone says.

"I wouldn't put up with all the bureaucracy if I were you," another says.

"As a Christian how can you teach in a public school?" yet another asks.

For some reason people believe that if it's hard, you should quit. Some Christians think if you can't spout Scripture from the front of the class, you shouldn't teach there. I disagree.

Why would Jesus tell us to endure hardship if it wasn't going to be hard? Why is there so much written in Scripture about perseverance if everything is supposed to go our way? Teaching is hard work, no doubt about it. If what happens in your school knocks you flat on your face in prayer, praise God! That means you're exactly where you're supposed to be—right where God can work with you.

Some equate the public schools with a mission field. This means that as teachers in the public schools, you are missionaries. There are times even missionaries take a sabbatical, so if you find yourself battling teaching fatigue and it affects your ability to teach, take a break. Then listen for the whisper of the Holy Spirit as He nudges you to return.

FINAL THOUGHT: No matter where you go or what you do—once a teacher, always a teacher.

Lord God, thank You for equipping me for this important ministry. Hold me up through the hardships, and give me strength to persevere.

239

DAY 120

A voice of one crying out:
Prepare the way of the LORD in the wilderness;
make a straight highway for our God in the desert.

ISAIAH 40:3

ALONE IN THE DESERT

Even when you teach in a school that has eight hundred students or more, you can still feel quite alone. Teachers sometimes isolate themselves, and that tendency only exacerbates any discouragement or frustration they might feel. While most of the time I caution against it, there are times when standing alone is the only choice, and one you are called to make.

I spent a lot of time as part of a staffing committee to place special-needs children in appropriate programs. There were times when after careful consideration I did not believe a particular child qualified for my learning-disabilities program. I did the evaluation. I met with the child and his parents. I wrote a report of my findings and recommendations. In the end he just didn't qualify for special services.

But there were times when my recommendation was overruled and the child was placed in the program against my judgment. I didn't want to label a child without cause. I stood alone.

We stand alone up in front of the class when we teach. We stand alone (or hopefully sit!) when we grade papers into the wee hours of the morning. And sometimes we stand alone in our convictions and beliefs. God's way of thinking isn't always easy for others to take. For most people it is contrary to their way of thinking and causes them to raise their fists against us. But we can stand on His Word, knowing that someday it will prepare the way for that Word to bring new life.

FINAL THOUGHT: When you must stand alone, stand tall.

Lord, if I am meant to stand alone, remind me that You are standing right there beside me.

DAY 121

With every prayer and request,
pray at all times in the Spirit, and stay alert in this,
with all perseverance and intercession for all the saints.

EPHESIANS 6:18

YOU PRAY FOR ME,
I'LL PRAY FOR YOU

How can we keep track of all those within our midst in need of prayer? Our students definitely need us to pray for them. Their parents could use the blessing of prayer as well. The other teachers we work with would benefit from sustaining prayer. We should pray for our legislative bodies who make decisions about education. If you made a list and prayed over the whole thing, you'd be praying all day!

With everything else we have to do, finding time to pray isn't a priority. After all, we have teaching to do, planning to do, conferences to hold, meetings to attend, reports to fill out, supplies to acquire, testing to conduct, papers to grade, report cards to turn in, and our own families to take care of. We barely have time to go to the bathroom, let alone set aside time to pray! Yet we must.

I can do everything on my to-do list without prayer, and it would be in vain. I must commit my work to His purposes, and the only way to do that is with prayer. Does it mean stop in your tracks and drop to your knees to pray? Not necessarily. Prayer can be a natural part of your daily activities. Pray over your class roster when you take attendance. Pray for the parent who left you a message that she needs to meet with you about her son. Pray for the teacher you see struggling to keep her students in line on their way to lunch. Pray for the legislators when you read in the paper about a new education initiative. We seem to find time to complain about these things. Choose to pray instead.

FINAL THOUGHT: Be on the hunt for prayer opportunities. They're all around you!

Lord, daily You provide me with opportunities to pray! Thank You for Your divine reminders to pray for those around me.

Pray also for me, that the message may be given to me when I open my mouth to make known with boldness the mystery of the gospel. For this I am an ambassador in chains. Pray that I might be bold enough in Him to speak as I should.

EPHESIANS 6:19–20

LIFE PRESERVERS

Sometimes we spend so much time ministering to the needs of others that we forget we have needs too. We advocate for students. We debate the value of one teaching approach over another. We stand our ground when parents try to intimidate us into taking a more subservient role. These are the things in which we are bold—we're the lifeguards of kids.

Lifeguards are well trained. They have to pass a battery of tests to see if they have what it takes to save lives. They have to be incredible swimmers, have quick reflexes, and keen powers of observation. No one ever expects lifeguards to need saving, but sometimes they do. As teachers we're not very good at reaching out when we're in need. We disconnect ourselves and slowly but surely fall into the depths of despair. We don't send up a flare. We don't even raise our arm to reach for the sky above us. We wonder why no one sees us drowning.

Like the apostle Paul, we can boldly ask for prayer. We can unashamedly reach out for the help we need. There's nothing to stop us except our pride. How privileged would a swimmer feel to come to the rescue of a lifeguard? Give people the opportunity to bestow acts of kindness and the blessings of prayer on someone they respect and admire—their teacher.

FINAL THOUGHT: Life preservers are only as effective as what they're tethered to—prayer is your lifeline to the Ultimate Lifeguard.

Lord, I can't do this job alone. I'm drowning! Open my mouth to ask for the help I need.

May He give you what your heart desires
and fulfill your whole purpose.
Let us shout for joy at your victory
and lift the banner in the name of our God.
May the LORD fulfill all your requests.

PSALM 20:4–5

YOU DON'T ALWAYS
GET WHAT YOU WANT

Life seems to be full of disappointments. Maybe you didn't get to teach in the school you wanted. Maybe your class this year is lopsided—more special-needs students than you anticipated; more discipline problems than in years past. Maybe you wanted to retire at the end of this year but now realize you can't afford to. Often we don't get what we want, but usually somehow, we get what we need.

The year I began teaching at a local college, I was sure it was exactly what I wanted. It would give me more flexibility in my schedule and availability to my family. But it was part time. Within a few months I started to feel the strain of less income and no benefits. I spent just as much time at this job as if it were full time, but without the pay and perks of full time. Was this a mistake? It sure began to feel like it.

At the same time we were struggling with our oldest son's school choices. His current high-school setting did not meet his needs. He needed a challenge that wasn't available where he attended. He lived in daily frustration and disappointment. At the pinnacle of my own aggravation, I discovered that because I was an employee of the college, my son could attend a new collegiate high school that was in partnership with the college.

It was a gift! Our son got what he needed, and although I still had some reservations about my job, I rested in the fact that I was exactly where I needed to be for reasons that were bigger than "I."

 FINAL THOUGHT: What you want may not always be what you need—or what others need.

Lord, show me the difference between wants and needs, and help me to be grateful for Your provision of both.

*For every high priest taken from men is appointed in
service to God for the people, to offer both gifts and
sacrifices for sins. He is able to deal gently with those
who are ignorant and are going astray,
since he himself is also subject to weakness.*

HEBREWS 5:1-2

NOT WHAT I SIGNED UP FOR

Teaching is a call to service, not a job opportunity.
When we answer that call, we're never quite sure
what we'll find when we show up. It's like signing our
names to the bottom of a contract that has yet to be
written. All God asks is that we come when He calls.

I stood at the front desk in a middle school waiting
to talk to the volunteer coordinator. She was busy, as
usual, on the phone and refusing to acknowledge my
presence at her desk. I'd taken time from my day to
drive fifteen miles out of my way to talk to this woman
about one of my college students who wanted to volunteer at the school. I stood there patiently, a smile pasted
to my face. I didn't want to make an enemy here; I just
wanted to advocate for my student.

After fifteen minutes of waiting and then finally having the conversation, it was clear I had no power. She was in charge, and the fact that I was a college professor who had previously taught at this middle school held no sway. I had to humble myself before her and basically beg that they allow my student to volunteer there. "Come back next week," she said. And all I could do was say, "Sure. No problem."

I walked through the vast acreage of the parking lot in the rain wondering why things that should be simple are so hard. I knew I'd drive back the next week, taking another hour out of my schedule. For a moment I questioned myself—why was I going to such lengths? But the answers were easy. I remembered what it's like to be an education major with no experience. My student needed me. And most importantly, this was part of my job, and hence, my calling from God.

FINAL THOUGHT: Teaching is a vocation, not an occupation.

Lord, I don't always know what I'll find when I answer Your call. But as Your child, I only know I need to come when I'm called.

*And whatever you do, in word or in deed,
do everything in the name of the Lord Jesus,
giving thanks to God the Father through Him.*

COLOSSIANS 3:17

DON'T BITE THE HAND THAT FEEDS YOU

The principal interviewed and hired me. The county pays me. The state collects the taxes that trickle into my paycheck. The taxpayers, well, it seems they're my real boss. Because of them I can feed my family.

If taxpayers at large are my boss, then should I work only to please them? It certainly feels that way much of the time. We continually bend to the will of the people. The people want school choice; we provide options. The people want safe schools; we install security cameras in the hallways and the bathrooms. The people want contained discipline; we create in-school suspensions and detentions. The people want to make sure kids eat breakfast; we offer breakfast at school. But teachers don't like being told what to do, so sometimes we balk at the demands of the people.

But as important as it is to appease the powers that be, it's more important to recognize that we work not to please people but to please God. This job at this school is provided to me not by the tax-payers, but by my Father in heaven. He is the reason I can feed my family. His purposes are the ones I fulfill as I teach every day. Focus first on the mighty hand of God. It's His hand that sustains your life and the lives of your students. He wants His children to be safe, to be fed, and get what they need. We can willingly run to meet those needs and be grateful for the chance to do so.

FINAL THOUGHT: Remember to thank, not bite, the hand that feeds you.

Lord, You alone are my provision. Forgive me for sometimes forgetting that truth.

He said, "I will cause all My goodness to pass in front of you, and I will proclaim the name Yahweh before you. I will be gracious to whom I will be gracious, and I will have compassion on whom I will have compassion."

EXODUS 33:19

COERCED COMPASSION

I remember a time in childhood when another kid sat on top of me and pinned my hands behind my back until they felt like they would break right off. It didn't take long for me to utter the word that would bring me relief: "Uncle!" The bully relented and walked away laughing. He showed mercy, but I was tortured first and forced to beg for it.

In the movies the bad guy is finally overpowered by the good guy and lies on the ground with a sword to his chest. The hero has every right to plunge the sword into his enemy yet shows mercy instead. Sometimes the villain repents in response to the mercy shown. Other times he walks away and says, "You should have killed me when you had the chance."

Our offering of mercy and compassion does not

depend on whether it is received. It is given freely without expectation of gratitude. Some students ask for a second chance, while others need one but never ask. The student who does everything in his power to thwart your authority still deserves your compassion. The student who isn't brave enough to ask for your help still deserves your mercy. We can let God's goodness pass in front of them by how we treat them.

God's compassion isn't about fairness; it's about His goodness. He can show compassion on whomever He wants. We don't have to agree with it. We can show compassion to whomever we want, and our students don't have to agree with it either. Just don't be like the bully who waits for his victim to say, "Uncle!" before showing that compassion.

FINAL THOUGHT: Being *moved* to compassion is different from being *forced* to compassion. Allow God to move you to the place where you will do the most good.

Lord, move me out of my complacency and into a place where I can show Your mercy and grace.

Moses immediately bowed down to the ground and worshiped. Then he said, "My Lord, if I have indeed found favor in Your sight, my Lord, please go with us. Even though this is a stiff-necked people, forgive our wrongdoing and sin, and accept us as Your own possession."

EXODUS 34:8-9

STICK-IN-THE-MUD

Do you ever find yourself advocating for those who refuse to change? I do that for students, but more often it's teachers whose stubbornness poses the greater challenge. Some of us are always on the hunt for a new and better way to teach and reach students. And when we discover a new tool or technique, we want to share it with others in hopes that they will share in our enthusiasm. What we find instead are crossed arms and expressionless faces. If it means more work or changing how they do things, they won't do it. If it means summoning up courage they just don't have, they won't do it.

New technology presents itself as a veteran teacher's greatest foe. It doesn't matter that the district requires they enter their grades on the computer—or that all school, parent, and district communication is conducted via e-mail—some teachers refuse to participate. This technology is outside their comfort zone, and it's like pulling a mule somewhere it doesn't want to go when you expect a teacher to change.

Yet, like Moses defending the stubborn Israelites, I am still called to stand up for them. I often find myself in the position of defending teachers to the general public. It's difficult for me to explain why teachers don't answer their e-mail or why the grades aren't entered in a timely fashion, especially when I know it's because they're stubborn.

I pray the Lord finds favor in what I do and forgives the teachers who are stubborn in their ways and thinking. It doesn't make me a martyr; it makes me an intercessor. Are you an advocate or an adversary to the profession?

FINAL THOUGHT: A stick-in-the-mud will either release itself and be pulled out or be broken off.

Lord, release me from my own imprisonment, and show me what I need to do to make a difference in my students' lives.

Humble yourselves therefore under the mighty hand of God, so that He may exalt you in due time, casting all your care upon Him, because He cares about you.

1 PETER 5:6–7

SCHOOL PRIDE

When I was a middle-school teacher, every Friday was spirit day. We'd wear our school T-shirts and walk around with spirit pins. We'd hoot and holler in the hallways about the upcoming varsity football game, and we'd strut our stuff along with the rest of the staff, trying to infuse excitement and pride in students who could otherwise be quite ambivalent. It didn't always work. Sometimes it felt like we just looked foolish for no reason. The kids still didn't seem to care.

But what is it we're really trying to say? Believing in your school is what it's all about? Allegiance to your team is the highest goal? If you polled teachers, they'd probably say they want to give students a sense of belonging and instill a sense of pride. Sounds reasonable, but I'm starting to think maybe we have the wrong goal. Pride comes before a fall—and the last thing kids need is another failure. Perhaps what they really need is a healthy dose of humility.

Maybe we should consider making every Friday *school-service day*. We can wear T-shirts that say, "Have you helped someone today?" and walk around with "I volunteer" pins. We can look for ways to encourage one another since most of us aren't the football players or cheerleaders. We can tally our volunteer hours as we serve one another and our communities, and we can offer others that much-needed pat on the back. Little by little, students will stop worrying about their own shortcomings. They'll discover community and watch in wonder as God works in their lives and those of their classmates. Excitement will finally edge out apathy as students replace false pride with genuine humility, allowing them for the first time to focus on others instead of themselves. Can you imagine it?

FINAL THOUGHT: The mighty hand of God deserves more praise than any high-school sports team!

Lord, the hand that feeds is more powerful than the hand that corrects, rebukes, or disciplines. Let my students see me as a model of service.

If I were you, I would appeal to God and would present my case to Him. He does great and unsearchable things, wonders without number.

JOB 5:8–9

DEAF EARS

Teachers tell their woes to anyone who will listen. The search for sympathy takes us outside of the teachers' lounge and into the line at the grocery store, onto the sidelines at our kid's soccer games, and beyond our borders in the close quarters of an airplane. We present our IDs to the cashier at the bookstore to get our educator discount and end up spilling our sorrows about the students who don't listen, the parents who don't care, and the principal who makes our job even harder than it has to be.

And nothing changes.

It seems our complaints fall on deaf ears. It's not that we're not explaining them right or saying them loud enough. The deaf can't hear. We're talking to the wrong people. They may be able to read our lips but can't do anything about what we say.

One of the things teachers learn quickly is who has the power in a school. It's not us. If something needs to change, we have to go to the source and plead our case. Sometimes it's the principal. Sometimes it's a supervisor or superintendent. But as we spin our wheels trying to get the right people to listen, we forget to take our case to the One whose sovereign power outweighs any school or district authority. Our God is the Almighty. Do you doubt what He can do for you? Do you know He is bigger than any problem you have with students, parents, or colleagues? It's one thing to find a sympathetic judge. It's quite another to find a sympathetic judge who actually has judicial power to change things. Our God is that judge.

FINAL THOUGHT: Plead your case to the only just Judge who has ears to hear.

Lord, I trust in Your judgment of me. Reveal to me what I lack so I might improve my skills to better meet the needs of my students.

259

See how happy the man is God corrects; so do not reject
the discipline of the Almighty. For He crushes but also
binds up; He strikes, but His hands also heal.

JOB 5:17–18

ASSESSMENT AND EVALUATION

The time of testing comes for all of us. Students experience testing year round. Over and over again their weaknesses are pinpointed, sometimes painfully so, and ways to improve are outlined. As adults we don't experience this constant assessment. When it happens, we are surprised, indignant, and sometimes hurt.

When that annual evaluation comes around and my principal or supervisor comes to my classroom with an observation form in hand, I sometimes feel as if she's on the hunt for me to mess up! She always finds what she's looking for—something I didn't do quite right. Maybe I didn't give enough specific praise. Maybe I ran out of time and forgot to conduct an ending review. Or maybe I didn't correct a student's behavior as quickly as I could have.

Have you ever been called into the principal's

office to go over your evaluation? You can feel just as small as a student does when he's sitting in that dreaded chair. Pointing out what's wrong is one thing. Offering a helping hand to correct it is something else. I realize that when I correct my students, I have to do much more than mark what's wrong on their papers. I need to offer a way for them to improve. I have to find ways to build them up. Otherwise, I crush their spirits.

When it comes to offering correction, I want to be as much like God as possible. He hates sin, but He certainly loves us! His Word points out our failings, but His love restores our souls. If my words consistently encourage rather than dishearten, maybe the next time I call a student to my desk to go over a test on which she did poorly, she will receive correction with a happier heart.

FINAL THOUGHT: Find a way to bundle correction with kindness—it's what makes the difference.

Lord, You lead me beside the still waters even in the midst of a storm. You are there with me in the middle of the fire. Let me walk with my students when they struggle too.

Again I saw under the sun that the race is not to the swift, or the battle to the strong, or bread to the wise, or riches to the discerning, or favor to the skillful; rather, time and chance happen to all of them.

ECCLESIASTES 9:11

RACING SCHOOL

You can learn a lot in racecar-driving school. You learn when to brake, when to accelerate, how to drive fast, how to stay safe, and how to keep three plastic balls in a bowl on the hood of the car while coming in under a certain target time. The best advice I got while I was there was to look ahead—not at the balls threatening to tumble off my hood. My hope was to drive smoothly. I didn't really care how fast I went. But it was racing school, so I guess the expectation was to go as fast as possible—safely.

A few of the hairpin curves threatened to curl my flat-ironed hair. There's an invisible perfect driving line on a race course. Finding the line and the balance it creates should be the goal, but I soon discovered it wasn't everyone's goal. Some barreled into the curves, panicked at their speed, and slammed on the brakes, releasing their now-weightless rear ends into the great unknown. They oversteered. Others approached the curves like slugs and then suddenly, as if realizing the embarrassment of their slow motion, mashed the throttle and drove right off the curve! They understeered.

Life throws us curves. I think about this as I evaluate my college students. I try to prepare them for the coming curves, but some run headlong into disaster. I can tell by where they place their focus. In racing school I was taught that your hands will steer where your eyes look. If you look at the wall, you're going to drive into the wall. It's true for our students as it is for us: we need to look as far ahead as we can when we navigate the course—yet keep our eyes on the road, not somewhere off in the clouds. If we take time to plan ahead for the curves, we won't be thrown off track when they suddenly come into view.

FINAL THOUGHT: The race set for us is won when we balance speed with caution. Keep your students' needs in sight as you navigate the course.

Lord, help me to look ahead so I might stay on track with my teaching.

Conduct yourselves honorably among the Gentiles, so that in a case where they speak against you as those who do evil, they may, by observing your good works, glorify God in a day of visitation.

1 Peter 2:12

The Great Conversation

Unfortunately, there tends to be a difference between what teachers *should* do and what they *actually* do. I often send my college students into the field to observe veteran teachers in the positions they hope to have themselves one day. Sometimes this is a discouraging exercise.

I teach them to review a child's IEP folder and familiarize themselves with the child's needs. But when they go into the schools, they hear, "I never look at the IEP folder. I don't need to change how I teach." I advise them to collaborate with other teachers to meet the needs of their students. They go to a school and run into closed doors and mouths. I instruct them to refer to children by name and not by their disability. They hear things like, "I'm glad I don't have any retards in my room this year." They come back to my class brokenhearted over what teachers don't do. This is where our real conversation begins.

When we run into those who don't do things the way they should, we have two choices. We can either use their negligence as an excuse for slacking off ourselves, or we can decide to do our best, no matter what. When we are doing quality work amidst others who aren't, we need to continue to treat others kindly and without judgment. That is, keep our words good, lovely, decent, amiable, and without blame. In the future, when those who dislike you (because you do what is right) are tempted to open their mouths in an unbecoming manner, they might think twice while in your presence. And who knows, it may be their first step toward a godly life. Behave honorably, regardless of what everyone else is doing, and you will bring glory to our Creator.

FINAL THOUGHT: Listen for ways to engage in conversation with your students that steer them to the truth.

Lord, let my words always bring glory and honor to Your Name. Help me to encourage my students to do the same.

"Lord," they said to Him, "open our eyes!"
Moved with compassion, Jesus touched their eyes.
Immediately they could see, and they followed Him.

MATTHEW 20:33–34

SEE A NEED, FILL IT!

Holes aren't usually good things. Holes in the road make driving miserable. Holes in windows let the mosquitoes in. Holes in our socks let our toes peek out when they should stay covered. Holes show where we're vulnerable. They must be filled.

A day at school is a day tiptoeing around holes. There are so many gaps, the fabric of school looks moth-eaten. Life moves so fast that we find ourselves only taking a cursory glance at the holes, even when they trip up our progress. When we sacrifice compassion for speed, the holes turn into chasms and threaten to swallow us all up.

What if our Lord walked through the crowds with blinders on, full of purpose on His way to the cross? The needs of the people He came to save must have overwhelmed Him as a man. They cried to Him to heal them, and He was moved to compassion. They followed the One who healed them—the One who stopped and filled the gaping holes in their souls.

Our students silently scream to us to see what they need in order to learn. Don't keep walking. Stop and fill their holes, and they will follow you.

FINAL THOUGHT: Teach in a way that fills holes rather than digs them deeper.

Lord, I know my own life is full of holes. Help me to remember You are the only One who can fill them.

*I pursue as my goal the prize promised
by God's heavenly call in Christ Jesus.
Therefore, all who are mature should think this way.*

PHILIPPIANS 3:14–15

BEST IN SHOW

I often wonder if middle- and high-school students have any sense of what they are working toward. We battle daily with their little-to-no motivation and scour the landscape for ways to spur them on to greatness. It feels more like we're poking them with cattle prods than instilling them with a sense of pride in their work. So many seem to settle for runner-up status; very few go for the gold. Maybe the reward isn't big enough. Maybe we expect too much. All I know is that they'll work pretty hard for ridiculously overpriced prizes from a magazine fund-raiser, yet they won't do what it takes to make the grade.

We live in a world where mediocrity is worthy of praise. Awards go to everyone, and being head of the class becomes a group denotation and not an individual achievement. We teachers can lose sight of the prize too. It's not easy to keep it in our vision when the battle to get through the school day takes all of our attention. Even when our gaze is fixed on excellence as a reward in itself, all it takes is the slightest movement in our peripheral view to take our eyes off the target. Kids are easily distracted, but teachers could use some self-regulated focus too.

Jesus set the standard. Our prize, the one we must set our sights on, is a life lived in fulfillment of the call to follow Him. Let us raise one another up, those who teach, in a way worthy of God's praise. Let us aspire to point others to the prize as well—students and fellow teachers.

FINAL THOUGHT: Keep your eye on the sparrow!

Unlike a butterfly that flits here and there, Your steadfastness is easy for my gaze to follow, Lord.

*And not only that, but we also rejoice in our afflictions,
because we know that affliction produces endurance,
endurance produces proven character,
and proven character produces hope.*

ROMANS 5:3-4

WHEN DOING WHAT'S RIGHT
SEEMS WRONG

Mr. Garcia, usually confident in his teaching, left his
principal's office questioning his abilities. He had
more grades below a C than any other teacher in the
entire school, and the principal wanted to know why.
Mr. Garcia knew he taught and graded a little differently than some of his colleagues; he just didn't think
the difference was that great! His grades for the nine
weeks fell into a natural bell curve. Those who found
themselves with an F on their report cards hadn't
done the work required. But Mr. Garcia squirmed
in his seat in his principal's office when his grades
and another science teacher's grades were compared
side by side. The other teacher didn't have any grades
below a B. How could that possibly be?

Throw-away assignments. Mr. Garcia's colleagues seemed to give a large number of assignments so easy that students would have to be asleep not to get a good grade on them. Why do this? How can you gauge student learning this way? You can't. (For that matter, how can you teach anything?) All it does is ensure a positive school image and satisfy the hunger of the No Child Left Behind bloodhounds sniffing around for students not achieving. But is it right?

Mr. Garcia didn't think so. He maintained his philosophy of teaching and didn't change his grades. He persevered through real persecution at his school, but knew from experience that at the end of the year his students would show real progress as they mastered the content. He had faith in them. Why didn't anyone else?

FINAL THOUGHT: Peer pressure comes from unexpected sources. Stay the course!

Lord, sometimes the pressure I feel is like a heaviness on my chest. Help me not to bend under its weight.

The Spirit Himself testifies together with our spirit that we are God's children, and if children, also heirs—heirs of God and co-heirs with Christ—seeing that we suffer with Him so that we may also be glorified with Him.

ROMANS 8:16–17

EASILY RECOGNIZABLE

During my first year of teaching I decided I didn't want to *look* like a teacher. My image of teachers was people who dressed for the decade in which they graduated from college and never moved on. They were out of style and hopelessly uncool. When you teach high school, students notice what you wear, and I did not want them snickering about me behind my back like they mocked other teachers. Unfortunately, in my attempts *not* to look like a teacher, I was mistaken for a student by teachers on more than one occasion. That didn't help my image at all.

How we look shouldn't be what identifies us as teachers. We have ID badges for that. I think others should know we're teachers by the words we use and the actions we take. The conversation that comes out of our mouths should be purposeful, uplifting, and for the good of kids. The steps we take should be carefully measured and aimed toward the success of students and harmony of faculty. Both ultimately bring glory to God. Both will lead us on the path of the cross as well.

Who I am in Christ is not determined by how I look on the outside. I know that positionally I am a child of God, and there are some identifiable characteristics that accompany that position. I will deny myself, take up my cross, and follow Christ. It is a path through suffering. I will be persecuted for His sake. Even as a teacher I do not escape this fate. The good news is that my ID badge is written on my heart and the Holy Spirit recognizes me from miles away. What I gain from suffering as a teacher does not begin to compare with the rewards waiting for me in glory!

FINAL THOUGHT: Persecution by society of a teacher is one thing. Persecution of a Christian teacher is another—the rewards for suffering are greater!

Lord, help me to hold on when the trial is greatest so others can see how it's done.

*It is honorable for a man to resolve a dispute,
but any fool can get himself into a quarrel.*

PROVERBS 20:3

REMEMBER WHAT YOU
MUST FORGET

What is it about us teachers that we hold on so tightly to those things that bother us the most? We hoard emotional insults like cherished treasures! A colleague disagrees with our position, and we take it personally. A parent complains about how we assign grades, and we let it create self-doubt. A student questions our authority, and we get defensive. Then we allow those things that bother us to determine how we treat others. We back off, lose our tempers, and sometimes lose control. In doing so, we lose what is most precious—our testimony.

There are days when it feels as if we have legions of opponents and no one is on our side. And yet God says, "Go forth!" Against impossible odds, He asks that we continue to teach even the most unlovable, unreachable souls. And you haven't quit yet, have you? But I wonder sometimes if we press on stoically rather than with the attitude He prescribes.

Is it obedience if we do what God has called us to but with a grumbling spirit and tongue? Our teaching message can get garbled, misunderstood, and even disconnected if not presented with love. What are the things that tie up the lines of communication in your teaching life? A sense of territory, a strong will, and sometimes a lack of compassion can make it impossible to get our message across to those who need to hear it the most. Identify the hindrances, bind them up, and give them to God. He will put them as far as the east is from the west. You can forget them. The only thing that will remain is love, and it is the one thing that makes communication crystal clear.

FINAL THOUGHT: After you clear up the lines of communication, ask, "Can you hear me now?"

Lord, I want to be constantly connected
to You so that I never miss what it is
You have to say to me.

Let your eyes look forward;
fix your gaze straight ahead.
Carefully consider the path for your feet,
and all your ways will be established.
Don't turn to the right or to the left;
keep your feet away from evil.

PROVERBS 4:25–27

EARPLUGS IN AND BLINDERS ON!

When I was first pregnant, everyone had a horror story to tell me about her pregnancy, labor, or delivery. I couldn't grasp why it was so important for them to relay to me all that went wrong. It scared me to death! My mother told me the best defense against this onslaught was to keep earplugs in and blinders on. I could just smile and nod my head in understanding but not allow myself to get caught up in their hysterics, or I'd quickly find myself in turmoil too.

It was good advice then for me as an expectant mother. It's good advice for me now as a teacher. Teachers are notorious for drawing others in. Like circling vultures, they target what's wrong with everyone and everything in school. If I allow them to circle, sooner or later they will drive me out of the field and then scavenge for whatever I've left behind.

The culture in which we work at school is fraught with ineffective communicators, territorial competitors, power-hungry politicians, and just plain angry people. It's not especially different from anywhere else in society. Somehow we expect it to be a more meaningful place to work—and it can be. We just have to learn how to do the job with earplugs in and blinders on.

I find that my eyes are diverted from the road when I see vultures circling above me. I crane my neck out the window to see what they are circling. Something is either dead or dying nearby. Unfortunately, when I allow myself to be distracted, I can end up veering right off the road! Stay focused on the task ahead so you don't end up as road kill.

FINAL THOUGHT: Keep your ears and eyes open only to truth.

Lord, bring Your truth to the foreground, and everything else will fall into the background.

But You Yourself have seen trouble and grief,
observing it in order to take the matter into Your hands.
The helpless entrusts himself to You;
You are a helper of the fatherless.

PSALM 10:14

ADOPTED FAMILY

Why is it that we refer to our students as our "kids"? I have to force myself to say "my students" when I talk about them to my family and friends. It's not something other people experience in their jobs. There's a familiarity to what we do—a connection that crosses unseen boundaries. Sometimes the familiarity blinds us; most times it makes us better teachers. If we treat our students "like family," we enfold them into our grace.

For some children their only source of stability and belonging comes from their teachers. School is a safe place compared to home. School is where they get at least two hot meals. School is where they don't have to worry about what comes next because its routine is predictable and comforting. Even children whose

278

lives are less chaotic appreciate what teachers offer them. We teach them so many things about how to get along in this world. Without what we offer, some would be helpless to find the success they want.

As a Christian you've been adopted into God's family—chosen and set apart as His heir and coheir with Christ. We are helpless without this adoption. We are rudderless without His loving direction. We are adrift without purpose and without preference. Our students are the same when they come to us. Can you view them as God sees them? These are His children that He has put in your care. Treat them as your own.

FINAL THOUGHT: Children shouldn't have to ask to be adopted. Choose them first.

Lord, my divine adoption was secure before the foundation of the earth. Let me make my students feel as if they've always belonged to me.

I searched for a man among them who would repair the wall and stand in the gap before Me on behalf of the land so that I might not destroy it, but I found no one.

EZEKIEL 22:30

STANDING IN THE GAP

Growing up, my brother viewed life through the lens of a severe learning disability. He was picked on more times than I can count, and he was not able to defend himself. He didn't have the words for a clever comeback when ridiculed. He didn't know how to deflect the less-than-honorable intents of his peers, and often either my sister or I stood between him and those who sought to harm him.

As a teacher there are times I must stand up for my students, when I have to open my mouth in their defense and stand guard in the hallways, in the school yard, and at the school's perimeter to keep them safe. As often as I am willing to do this, I find myself in need of the same type of advocacy. But who will stand for me?

Public education is under constant attack. We

are bombarded by ideologies that wish to destroy us, critics who intend to devalue us, and the intolerant who want nothing more than to homogenize us. The world sits in judgment on a system in which they refuse to participate. They are part of the problem. I keep waiting for someone to choose to be a part of the solution, but I fear I'm wasting my time.

We need to stand up for one another. We need to defend one another's honor, encourage one another's commitment, and soothe one another's spirits. God is calling out to us to stand in the gap. You may feel it's impossible for one person to hold his hand against a flood, but it's time to stand in the gap and be part of the solution to education problems.

FINAL THOUGHT: Moses didn't hold back the waters of the Red Sea by himself. But with God's outstretched hand, he stood between doom and delivery. You can too.

Lord, hold my hand as I hold the hands of other teachers, and let Your power flow through us all.

He will not cry out or shout
or make His voice heard in the streets.
He will not break a bruised reed,
and He will not put out a smoldering wick;
He will faithfully bring justice.

ISAIAH 42:2–3

FAIRNESS AND LIGHT

"Colin!" Miss Jenny called from across the room. "I told you to sit down!"

Two minutes later.

"Colin!" Miss Jenny yelled from her desk. "I told you to keep your hands in your own space!"

Three minutes later.

"Colin!" Miss Jenny stood over the repeat offender and raised her voice once again. "Go sit in time-out until you decide you can stay on task!"

Colin sat in time-out until lunch.

Miss Jenny seemed to have an eagle's eye when it came to Colin, but somehow she never saw Sarah cutting up her assignment sheet with the scissors she never returned, or Michael scuttle under his desk picking up an imaginary pencil he claimed he dropped. She didn't see Melissa sharpening her pencil until it was a stub and not doing her seatwork.

But Colin did see what Miss Jenny missed and wasn't too happy about it. He sat in time-out watching everyone else get away with whatever they were doing. *Not fair!* he thought.

There are those in our classrooms who constantly give us trouble that we can see and hear. All we want to do is stamp out their behavior. But we have to remember that many children are already bruised souls. Breaking them completely does nothing to restore them. We are called to bring life into the lives of the children in our care. We can treat them with fairness, administer appropriate discipline, and still be a light in the darkness to them.

FINAL THOUGHT: Those who need you the most are often the ones most difficult to deal with.

Lord, I'm guilty of tunnel vision when it comes to my students. Replace my narrow view with one that has a wider lens.

[Instruct them] to do good, to be rich in
good works, to be generous, willing to share,
storing up for themselves a good foundation
for the age to come, so that they may
take hold of life that is real.

1 TIMOTHY 6:18–19

EASY COME, EASY GO

I sent my college students out into the schools to do observation hours and gather information that would help them become better teachers after graduation. They were dumbfounded by the lack of generosity they encountered.

"I couldn't get anyone to show me the forms they use to document problem behaviors," more than one reported.

"Even with parent permission they wouldn't let me view the child's special-education folder," at least eight students complained.

"They wouldn't let me sit in on a faculty meeting," a few shared. "What is this—a secret society or something?"

It certainly makes you wonder what we're hiding. I'd like to tell them that normally teachers are generous people, but it just isn't true. We're territorial at best and adversarial at worst. We close our doors and sometimes our hearts to adults who might need our help. We're good at giving students what they need, but parents, other teachers, and even soon-to-be teachers seldom experience our generous spirits.

The gifts and opportunities we've been given as teachers are not for us to hoard and hide. They are for us to give away, heaping blessings on those we encounter on a day-to-day basis. We're all here for the same reason: to reach and teach students. To make a difference in their lives. We can have the greatest impact when we pool our resources and give of ourselves to all who ask.

FINAL THOUGHT: Whatever gifts you've been given are in your hands only as long as it takes you to give them away.

Lord, loosen my grip so I can gladly give away the gifts You've given me.

For we are His creation—created in Christ Jesus for good works, which God prepared ahead of time so that we should walk in them.

EPHESIANS 2:10

BEST-LAID PLANS

What does it mean to teach by the seat of your pants? It usually means you didn't write a lesson plan and didn't prepare ahead of time what you wanted your students to learn. Some teachers, beginners and veterans, believe their creativity is stifled if they have to "plan" their lessons. They reason that learning is enhanced by a more spontaneous environment. Makes me wonder what they think about the way their Creator does business.

We have a God of order and purpose. He does nothing without a plan! There is more creativity in His design than we can possibly imagine. Look around at His handiwork and see for yourself! His plans may not be revealed to us as we go through His lessons, but they exist nevertheless. We can plan for our students in the same way. They don't have to see the inner workings of how we prepare for them, but they can reap the benefits of our preparedness.

Nothing is a surprise to God. He has considered those things that might cause us to stumble. And He always has a contingency plan in place. When we plan for our students, we must think about what difficulties they might experience during the lesson and then plan in a way that anticipates those difficulties. Our plans should be less about us and more about them. Ultimately, their successes will reflect well on our teaching. Plan for that success right from the beginning.

FINAL THOUGHT: Creativity doesn't come out of chaos; it comes from design.

Lord, thank You for reminding me about the satisfaction that comes from following a well-thought-out plan.

For I may be absent in body,
but I am with you in spirit,
rejoicing to see your good order
and the strength of your faith in Christ.

COLOSSIANS 2:5

TAKING ATTENDANCE

Schools cringe when you call in sick as a teacher. In most other jobs your absence doesn't cause such a ruckus. The greatest fear from your principal is "when the cat's away, the mice will play!" And often that's exactly what happens—student behavior goes down the tubes when the regular teacher is absent. Is a solution a matter of having a well-trained substitute in your place? I don't think so.

As parents we know that the way our children behave in the care of others when we're not around is a testimony of our parenting. Often our kids will behave better for other people than they will for us. They don't behave out of fear that we'll punish them, but instead out of love for us and respect for the values we've taught them. It works the same for teachers and students.

When you're absent from school, your spirit should still be present in the classroom. Students will behave out of love for you and respect for the values you've taught them. They will listen to the substitute and do the right things in anticipation of your praise. Students should know you look forward to being proud of them upon your return. Teach them well, and they will make you proud in your absence.

FINAL THOUGHT: Students' behavior for the substitute doesn't depend on the substitute. It depends on your teaching.

Just as I hope You are pleased with me when You return, Jesus, help me to instill the same desire in my students.

*Then He said, "Woe also to you experts in the law!
You load people with burdens that are hard
to carry, yet you yourselves don't touch these
burdens with one of your fingers."*

LUKE 11:46

INSTRUCTIONAL LEADERSHIP

Raise your hand if you are overwhelmed with policies and procedures and all the paperwork that goes with them. How many feel your teaching is strangled by recent federal legislation? OK, most of you. How many of you wish those who make up all these rules would spend one day teaching in your classroom to get a clue about what it takes to even begin to jump through all these hoops? I see an ocean of hands in the air even from where I sit.

Why does it seem that when people go into leadership positions in the school system (all the way up to the federal level), they forget what it's like to teach in the classroom? The problem is that many of those who make the rules have *never* spent one day as a teacher in the classroom. Unfortunately, this makes it difficult for teachers to follow them willingly.

Here's what I love about Jesus. He humbled Himself to be born a man, suffered in the trenches, died, overcame death, and then asked us to follow Him for our good and His glory. He knows what our life is like, and that alone motivates me to follow His lead. His burden is light. Why? Because He's carrying most of it for us. How many administrators and legislators can you say that about?

An instructional leader is someone who leads in a school by first modeling what he expects and then supports you as you do it on your own. If you find yourself in a leadership position, even as a department head or committee leader, take your cue from the greatest Instructional Leader of all.

FINAL THOUGHT: You have to prove you know where you're going before someone will follow you willingly.

Lord, let me show my students I know what their lives are like, so they will follow my lead more willingly.

So if one member suffers, all the members suffer with it;
if one member is honored, all the members rejoice with it.

1 CORINTHIANS 12:26

ALL FOR ONE AND ONE FOR ALL

Team teaching is a concept that's been around for a long time. Now in the spirit of cooperation we are working toward an even more cohesive teaching arrangement. Collaboration and the inclusive classroom seek to support the needs of all children taught together. As we work to raise the awareness and sensitivity of students to work collectively and learn to appreciate one another's gifts and talents, we find ourselves learning to do the same with one another as educators.

Take a general-education teacher and pair him with a special-education teacher. One is an expert on content; the other, on strategies. Create a classroom combination of students with a variety of learning styles and needs. Then allow the teachers to each do what he or she does best, and watch as what was once a divided class becomes one united class, each group learning from the other. It's a recipe for success for all involved. Teachers who once felt ill-equipped are supported, and those who felt alienated are now a part of the whole. This relationship is mirrored in the students themselves. They realize, maybe for the first time, that they are a part of something bigger than themselves.

As members of the body of Christ, we, too, can experience the joy that comes when one of our members succeeds in his or her calling. And since we are all teachers, we can also be a part of their suffering when it arrives. When a student struggles, we all struggle with him. And when a student finally succeeds, we all rejoice with him. Let our collaboration in the classroom mimic the collaboration of the Father, the Son, and the Holy Spirit!

FINAL THOUGHT: God's kingdom is the most successful inclusive classroom!

Lord, help me to be willing to collaborate for the sake of my students.

293

*For I want very much to see you, that I may
impart to you some spiritual gift to strengthen you,
that is, to be mutually encouraged
by each other's faith, both yours and mine.*

ROMANS 1:11–12

BE ENCOURAGED

Sometimes as teachers we feel like we've come to the end of ourselves, and yet we're still expected to pour ourselves out as from an empty vessel. We give and we give and we give, and out of the dried cracks of our emptiness, we give some more. So when another teacher needs encouragement or assistance, we sometimes hesitate as if measuring the reward. Will it help me if I help her? Will helping take too much out of me? Will my assistance go unappreciated and unnoticed like it does with my students? If her need is great, I may be tempted to slowly back away, like a camper trying to stay downwind of a bear. We count the cost, and sometimes the cost is too high.

As you read this right now, you're probably aware of at least one other teacher in your faculty who is struggling. You've seen her. You know she hasn't "officially" asked for help. Do you think it's a co-incidence that her need has been revealed to you? I guarantee that you have something she needs. It may be a friendly word; it may be a strategy; it may be a helping hand. God reveals to us those who need our encouragement. And He doesn't do it only for their sakes. He does it for ours.

In giving, you will receive. In encouraging, you will be encouraged. Acts of mercy and kindness minister just as much to the giver as to the receiver. So just when you think you have nothing left to give, God asks you to give some more. Jesus poured Himself out for us on the cross. He gave until it killed Him. We can give until it hurts and still never come close to the mercy and kindness of our Lord.

FINAL THOUGHT: No pain, no gain. No truer words were ever spoken.

Lord, help me to be a blessing to others, and in that way I will be blessed.

Stop judging according to outward appearances;
rather judge according to righteous judgment.

JOHN 7:24

BEST FIRST IMPRESSIONS

She was prepared, well prepared, for her interview. Shellie graduated at the top of her class, and her resume boasted of leadership experiences, extra teaching duties, and child-advocacy group involvement. Primed and ready to take responsibility for a class of her own, Shellie had communication skills that made the interviewing principal sit up and take notice. But he noticed more than her expertise. All it took was a twist of her heel and a sideways glance from the principal to kill her dream.

"Miss Stanley," he began. "There's some sort of smudge on your ankle. You must have rubbed your foot up against something." He rose to offer her a tissue.

"Oh, that," Shellie said. "That's not a smudge. It's just my tattoo. Thanks for taking the time to meet with me, Mr. Reynolds. I look forward to hearing from you soon."

Shellie never heard back from Mr. Reynolds. Unfortunately, the smudge on her ankle was a deal breaker.

We all find ways to judge each other. Sometimes how well we do our jobs is eclipsed by a smudge on the ankle, a sparkling diamond nose stud, or a Harley in the faculty parking lot. It isn't right, but it is reality. What can we learn from this? Reserve judgment about other teachers or parents for the grounds of righteousness and not outward appearance.

FINAL THOUGHT: Be careful how you judge. You will be judged by others the way you judge them.

Lord, You are the only just Judge. Thank You for reminding me that judging is not a part of my job description.

Encourage the young men to be sensible about everything. Set an example of good works yourself, with integrity and dignity in your teaching.

TITUS 2:6–7

BOYS WILL BE BOYS

Studies in the past suggested that teachers pay more attention to boys than girls in the classroom. They call on them more. They offer assistance more often. But studies also show that more boys than girls offer disciplinary problems. The attention we give them isn't always for positive reasons. The old adage is true—the squeaky wheel gets the oil. My own boys usually made an impression on the teachers they had in one way or another.

How can we encourage our young men to learn positive behaviors and strive for excellence when it seems so many of them just don't care? Our teaching becomes reactionary and doesn't offer them a path to follow. We can do better by first exemplifying the traits we value and hope to instill in them. The best-case scenario would be for more male teachers to offer this all-important modeling, but since at least 85 percent of grade-school teachers are female, we can't wait for more male teachers; we must try harder to reach these boys ourselves. They may not be as organized as girls, but we can show them how to be. Some may struggle to stay on task, but we can help them focus. Others may forget how to speak respectfully, but we can teach them. The integrity and dignity we model will speak volumes to kids. Even if you realize late in the year that you've neglected that responsibility, you can begin right now. It is never too late to start doing the right thing.

FINAL THOUGHT: Boys will someday be men. Show them now how to treat others by the way you treat them.

Lord, even Your mother worried about where You were and what You were doing. But she followed up and found You. Help me to stay watchful of all the children in my care.

DAY 150

Since I am confident of your obedience,
I am writing to you, knowing that
you will do even more than I say.

PHILEMON 21

COUNTDOWN TO SHUT DOWN

Have you already begun your end-of-the-year countdown? Some of us start it earlier than others, usually in response to our weariness. Being in countdown mode shows us we're close to the end of the school year. But something else tends to happen when we enter countdown mode. We begin to shut down. Some of us have already started summer break in our minds, even though our bodies still occupy our desks.

The assignments and activities we give students also indicate our countdown mode. They're fewer, shorter, and easier to grade. True, there may be some stray semester-long projects we still need to collect and grade, but anything else we assign will be easy on us and easy on them. We've fallen into the trap of doing only the bare minimum to get by!

300

I offer you a challenge. Instead of counting down to shut down, count down to blast off! You're at the point in the school year where you really need your second wind. You've been running a marathon, and now it's time to tap into your reserves and sprint toward the finish line. Make your last lessons the best ones. Spend more time, not less, working one-on-one with students. Increase your planning to make the coming end of this school year satisfying for all of you. Do more than expected!

FINAL THOUGHT: Even now we can still learn from the Little Engine That Could. Full steam ahead!

Lord, renew my spirit so I might continue forward with refreshed purpose and energy.

The goal of our instruction is love from a pure heart, a good conscience, and a sincere faith. Some have deviated from these and turned aside to fruitless discussion. They want to be teachers of the law, although they don't understand what they are saying or what they are insisting on.

1 TIMOTHY 1:5–7

ALL TALK, ALL THE TIME

I love having philosophical and ethical discussions with my college students about teaching. They are so idealistic and willing to do whatever it takes to impact the lives of children. Their motivation is pure. They want to do the right thing, and they believe they can. They are not afraid to speak up about what students need to succeed and their own innovative ideas for improving education.

But the culture of many schools fosters a different kind of conversation. Once we get into teaching positions, prideful human nature rears its ugly head, and we want to be the rule makers and rule enforcers. We talk about ways to work around the system to get what we want. We grumble about how the job is affecting our families, ruining our sleep, and keeping us from financial prosperity. We forget this job isn't really about us—it's about the children. Why is it so hard to maintain that perspective? We discuss how invasive the state and federal governments are becoming. We gripe about how ineffective our union is in getting us a much-deserved and long-awaited pay raise. We look suspiciously at anyone who wants to come observe us in our classrooms, and we curse the open-door policy the principal propagates to parents.

All our negative talk hinders the case for Christ. The way our tongues wag, you wouldn't think we live, work, and play in the shadow of the wings of an almighty God. We have so much to teach those students placed in our care. It's up to us to shift the conversation toward those things that are true and of good report. We can be examples to our students and a breath of fresh air to our colleagues by keeping our words dignified and above reproach.

FINAL THOUGHT: If you can't silence pointless discussion with your words, take your words somewhere else.

Father, guard my lips so I might speak only those words that glorify You.

He must seek peace and pursue it,
because the eyes of the Lord are on the righteous
and His ears are open to their request.

1 PETER 3:11–12

FINDERS KEEPERS

I remember the first time I went fishing. We lived near a beautiful pier that was front-row center to glorious sunrises and welcomed manatees to its edge—but unfortunately, no fish. I decided fishing was boring and couldn't fathom why anyone in her right mind would enjoy such a pursuit. I did catch a couple of crabs as they annoyingly stole the bait off my line.

"I've been here for three hours and not one bite," I complained to the boy next to me pulling up his crab traps that were bursting with life.

"If you want to catch fish, you need to go where the fish are," he said.

What a concept! "And where's that?" I asked.

"Over toward that inlet south of here," he

pointed to a craggy shoreline next to a nest of mangrove trees.

The next time, I went where the fish were and finally caught some. But it took more than their nibbling the bait for me to reel them in. First, I had to find them. I had to pursue them. I had to struggle to bring them into my net. You don't catch fish by waiting for them to hook themselves!

Peace is like that. It doesn't come knocking on your door, saying, "Here I am. Claim me!" First, we need to go to the One in whose presence peace resides. Then we need to pursue it, sometimes with a struggle, and then bring it into our hearts. If you want peace in your classroom, actively seek God's peace, track it down, then hold on to it for dear life!

FINAL THOUGHT: Be on the hunt for peace. If you find it, you can keep it!

Lord Jesus, You are the source of my peace. Teach me to pursue You relentlessly so I might have Your peace and pass it on.

DAY 153

This came from the LORD;
it is wonderful in our eyes.
This is the day the LORD has made;
let us rejoice and be glad in it.

PSALM 118:23–24

ALL GOOD THINGS

The lesson went smoothly. My students caught what I taught them and giggled at their new understanding. I smiled because I know what it takes for some of them to grasp concepts and applauded their diligence and success. Discipline problems were absent, although all my students were present. I surveyed my class and watched as the groups worked cooperatively and the noise hovered at a pleasant buzz. This was good. This was very good.

Whom do you thank when things go right? When your supplies show up intact, do you thank the bookkeeper? When no one misbehaves, do you thank the parents? When a struggling student finally "gets it," do you thank your expertise? You can, but

306

it's not enough. Every good and perfect thing comes from God. He is the Author of good.

On *our* good days, the ones for which we find no complaint, we can rejoice! Sometimes we forget to be thankful when things are going well. We ignore God in the easy times; we only remember to cry to Him in the difficult. God makes each and every day. What we do with those days is up to us. But each and every day He makes is good, and we should thank Him for them.

Even on those days when everyone misbehaves and everything goes wrong, we can still thank God for that day. When He made it, it was good. What we do with it, how we respond to it, and how we organize it is up to us.

FINAL THOUGHT: Thank the Lord for He is good—and so is all He creates!

Father, I thank You now for this day. It is good!

Day 154

*Plans fail when there is no counsel,
but with many advisers they succeed.*

PROVERBS 15:22

TEAM MEETINGS

When kids first learn how to play baseball, they inevitably bump heads. Even though it's a team sport, a lot depends on individual performance. He has a strong arm—let's put him in at third base. His throw hits the bull's-eye every time—let's make him our pitcher. He sure can catch those high flies—put him in left field. Everyone has a job to do, and all are encouraged to "call the ball" when it comes their way. Some call a catch before they're ready, and the other players stand back and wait. The overconfident lug is nowhere near the ball when it hits the dirt. Others call it when it's not within their reach, disregarding the territory of another player. Both run for the ball, smash heads, and neither catches it. These are errors. They can cost the team the game.

One of the things teachers struggle to do well is work as a team. Ironically—since we're all members

308

of more teams, committees, and faculties than we can count—some of us are lone rangers. We tend to do everything by ourselves and without help. Some of us rush into areas for which we're not quite equipped and bump heads with those who are trained for the task at hand. Others offer to take responsibility, yet never follow through. These are errors in teaching. And they can cost students' optimal learning opportunities.

When you're faced with something you don't know how to handle, seek wise counsel. There are others who have wisdom you need. Depend on your team—a pitcher is no good without a catcher, and they're both ineffective without infielders and out-fielders. (Not to mention a coach!) Going it alone helps no one. When you find yourself banging your head against the wall, remember there's someone just on the other side who can help.

FINAL THOUGHT: A meeting of the minds is so much more productive than a butting of the heads.

Lord Jesus, thank You for surrounding me with a team. Remind me to rely on them for counsel, and help me to be a supportive advisor when needed.

*Though he falls, he will not be overwhelmed,
because the LORD holds his hand.*

PSALM 37:24

LIFTED UP

I learned how to ski when I was thirty-eight—sort of. I had visions of swooshing down the white-powdered slopes with the grace of a gazelle. I should have gotten the hint this wasn't as easy as it looked when the first thing they taught me in ski school was how to fall.

Falling, as it turned out, wasn't that difficult to do. Getting up, on the other hand, was nearly impossible as far as I was concerned! After leaning on people stronger than I to inch my way up from the cold ground, I was ready to conquer the mountain. The biggest problem was at the top of the slope. You have to actually get off the ski lift before you can ski! Much to my dismay, I could never do that gracefully. I fell flat on my face each and every time!

The humiliation was bad enough, but couple it with a less-than-patient ski-lift dude, all of nineteen years old, who took sadistic pleasure in screaming at people as they sunk deeper into the snow, and you get me—a crying snow baby. I fell over and over again, and he yelled at me over and over again. Finally, my youngest son, nine years old, came to help me back onto my feet. The next time I tried the lift, he held my hand when we slid onto the waiting snow. I still fell, but this time someone who cared about me held my hand.

There are students in your class who've been humiliated when they didn't understand, who aren't steady on their feet, and who have given up altogether at this point. They're still probably going to fall, but maybe you could be the one to hold their hands when they do.

FINAL THOUGHT: Even if you know they're going to fall, stand hand in hand with your students. That way you'll be right there to help them back onto their feet.

Thank you, Lord Jesus, for holding my hand when I fall.

*To God we are the fragrance of Christ among those who
are being saved and among those who are perishing.
To some we are a scent of death leading to death,
but to others, a scent of life leading to life.*

2 Corinthians 2:15–16

What's That Smell?

I sat on the floor of the black-and-white tiled bathroom and leaned my cheek against the cool wall, hoping for some relief. Since I'd already stuffed a towel into the crack under the door, I could only hear the muffled sounds of my family in the kitchen. They sounded happy enough, but the knocking of pots and pans told me they weren't even close to being done yet. Finally, my curiosity got the best of me, and I removed the towel to hear what they were saying.

"That smells incredible," I heard my husband say. "How much garlic did you use, anyway?"

That was all I needed to hear. I rammed the towel back and thrust open the bathroom window. I stuck my head out and gulped the cool lake air. How could a nice Italian girl have such an aversion to the smell of garlic when she's pregnant? Garlic smells like garlic. To the rest of my family the aroma was heavenly. To me it was the aroma of . . . well, you really don't wnat me to tell you.

You can only offer students yourself, your expertise, and your compassion. You offer the same to everyone—it's all you've got! But it doesn't mean the "aroma" will be pleasant to all of your students. There will be some who salivate and devour what you've taught them. But then there will always be a few who run from your teaching as if from a pile of green vegetables! Just make sure that what you have to offer them has the scent of Jesus on it. Don't alter its composition or cover it up with some other perfume. Let them catch a whiff of Him as He is, and let them decide for themselves if they want more.

FINAL THOUGHT: If you eat garlic, you'll smell like garlic. If you ingest Jesus, you'll smell like Him too.

Lord, infuse me with Your aroma that I might have a pleasing scent to share with my students.

Command and teach these things. No one should despise your youth; instead, you should be an example to the believers in speech, in conduct, in love, in faith, in purity. . . . Do not neglect the gift that is in you.

1 Timothy 4:11–12, 14

New Teachers

The dispositional and ethical issues new teachers face surprise and discourage them. Sometimes they cause them to leave the profession much sooner than any of us expect. As I supervise student teachers in the schools, I notice one of the things that frustrates them is the way some veteran teachers look down their noses at them. They are quickly criticized for what they are—young and inexperienced.

They're taken for granted and asked to do things the older, more experienced teachers won't do. Every little misstep is pointed out as an unforgivable offense. *You didn't paper-clip the students' assignments before putting them on my desk (yet they're in a nice, neat pile). You forgot to wipe down the desks with antibacterial cleanser at the end of the day like I do. (I didn't realize I was the custodian too.) You should have parked in the back of the lot so you don't take someone's permanent spot (not that they're labeled or anything).*

Even a veteran teacher who moves to a new school faces the "I've been here longer than you" tribunal. It's certainly a challenge to fit in and follow a new routine. Sometimes you don't know what the rules are until you break them. How does a new teacher do her best work and remain upbeat under such adversarial conditions?

Remember your calling. You've been given the gift of teaching. Use it even in the face of those who may oppose you. Make sure your attitude and behavior are above reproach. Teach in a way that makes obvious your love, faith, and purity.

FINAL THOUGHT: We've all been the "new" teacher. Train them up in the way they should go, but do it in a way that builds up and doesn't tear down.

Lord, enable me with Your patience, compassion, and grace when I interact with those less experienced than I. After all, You treat me like that every day!

*I am not conscious of anything against myself, but
I am not justified by this. The One who evaluates me
is the Lord. Therefore don't judge anything prematurely,
before the Lord comes, who will both bring to light
what is hidden in darkness and reveal
the intentions of the hearts.*

I Corinthians 4:4–5

Evaluation Time

The activities of both teaching and learning include a multitude of evaluations. We grade students on their learning. We judge parents based on their involvement. We assess other faculty members. We're asked to be reflective teachers and evaluate our own attitudes and abilities. Evaluations are often worthy pursuits, but how we perform in an assessment changes with every moment in time. We are all works in progress. Even when students graduate from high school, they are only on the beginning of their journeys.

It's difficult in the culture of school to accept that we are all in the process of learning. Students squirm when we give them room to grow. They want to know whether they gave the right answer at the right time and in the right way. There's a learning continuum, and we're all at a different spot.

Even when we assess ourselves, we don't see clearly. We try to "self correct," but it often takes someone else to show us where we need to improve. Even then, we can only take one step at a time.

You may be discouraged by your performance on some teaching task. Maybe you're not as organized as you need to be. Maybe you still struggle with student discipline. Maybe your transitions are jerky or hard for kids to follow. You are a work in progress. God is your judge. Offer yourself up to Him, and He will reveal to you what you must do to improve. Allow Him that privilege.

FINAL THOUGHT: Even after someone has been taught, they are still learning.

Father, give me patience with all the "works in progress" around me—and give them patience with me!

Day 159

*Now to Him who is able to do above and beyond all
that we ask or think—according to the power that
works in you—to Him be glory in the church and in
Christ Jesus to all generations, forever and ever. Amen.*

Ephesians 3:20–21

Power Holders

I try to prepare new teachers for the real world in
our orientation sessions. There are things they didn't
learn in their courses that will profoundly affect
their teaching experience. I tell them how important
it is to get to know the culture of their schools. Each
school has its own traditions, ways of communicat-
ing, and power holders. Those who hold the power
aren't always obvious at first. And those with the
power tend to try to make the rest of us feel powerless. Head custodians, the lunch ladies, and the principal's secretary all have power that can surprise us.

No matter who has the power, there are limits
to what they can do. The custodian can vacuum your
classroom, but he can't seem to get the throw-up stain
out of the carpet. The cafeteria manager can give you

extra portions, but she can't change the menu for you if you're lactose intolerant. And the principal's secretary can get you on the principal's calendar, but she can't turn the other way if you come in late because your daughter's babysitter didn't show up on time.

The problem comes when we *believe* that those with perceived power have real power. They have whatever power we give them, real or not. The only one who truly has the power to change lives is almighty God! His Spirit breathes His will into those He has called. Do you realize that His power resides in you? Inside of you is the power to do more than expected—to save lives, and to shape them? You have more real power in your little pinky than any school leader's army of servants. You can change lives because you have the greatest Change Agent living right inside of you!

FINAL THOUGHT: The enemy wants you to believe you're powerless because he's afraid of the power of Christ that resides in you. Tap into that power today!

Lord Jesus, I can stand sure knowing Your power flows through me.

DAY 160

*Do not rebuke an older man, but exhort
him as a father, younger men as brothers,
older women as mothers, and with all propriety,
the younger women as sisters.*

1 TIMOTHY 5:1-2

WE ARE FAMILY

As Christian teachers we live as part of the household of faith. And as such we relate to one another as family. All families are dysfunctional here on earth. We won't relate like coheirs with Christ until we live together with Him in heaven. For now we need to focus our efforts on relating in a manner worthy of our calling. And that can be quite a challenge when you're part of a teaching faculty.

There are those who've been doing this much longer than you have, and often their lack of flexibility can frustrate you. There are those who have just joined the family, and their beginner mistakes annoy you to no end. Each needs your support and respect, even when all you want to do is distance yourself from them. Can you offer correction and respect while

320

encouraging them to improve their teaching? You have to.

The truth spoken in love works for those both within and without the faith. But it cannot be spoken outside of a relationship. Befriend the older, more experienced teacher, and develop a measure of understanding and respect for what he has already accomplished as a teacher. Only then can you approach him with suggestions or criticism. Spend time, as you would with a brother or sister, with the teacher who is younger than you, and let him learn by watching. To that one, you are someone to look up to. Make it an intriguing and encouraging show and tell!

FINAL THOUGHT: Education is all about relationship—and so are families. As a faculty you are a part of both.

Lord, thank You for this family You've provided me. Let me treat them with the respect and love they deserve.

DAY 161

*Let brotherly love continue. Don't neglect to show
hospitality, for by doing this some have welcomed
angels as guests without knowing it.*

HEBREWS 13:1–2

IN OUR MIDST

There are not enough substitutes to go around.
School secretaries panic when they get the dreaded,
"I can't come in today" phone call just before the
start of school. Some schools are so desperate, they
implore interns and even parents to step into the
gaping hole of a teacher's absence. The irony is that
once a substitute gets to the school, she can feel anything but welcome. She certainly isn't treated like a
lifesaver.

Instead of extending our hands in welcome, we
eye her suspiciously when she enters the teachers'
lunchroom. It's high school all over again, and we
somehow make available seats "unavailable" at the
last moment. We don't make eye contact with this
stranger. And we certainly don't start a conversation
with her. This may not happen at every school, but

I know plenty of substitutes and have held the job myself for enough time to know it is true in *many* schools.

I can't help but hear the Lord's words in my head when I consider this situation. "Whatever you did for one of the least of these brothers of Mine, you did for Me" (Matthew 25:40). We tend to view substitutes like the least of our brothers (or sisters). Why don't we treat them better? Not only should we strive to show hospitality so they will prefer to substitute at our school again in the future, but also because you never know who they are and who they know.

Welcome that substitute to your table. Offer her assistance, and make yourself available in case she needs help during the school day. Who knows? She could be an angel in disguise!

FINAL THOUGHT: Make sure you take the time to recognize the angel in your midst.

Father, forgive me for all the times I ignore or disrespect others whom you've placed in front of me. Open my eyes to those who need a kind word or helping hand.

*My brothers, hold your faith in our glorious Lord Jesus
Christ without showing favoritism. . . . Listen, my
dear brothers: Didn't God choose the poor in this world
to be rich in faith and heirs of the kingdom
that He has promised to those who love Him?*

JAMES 2:1, 5

RAGGEDY ANDY

It's early in my career, and I'm teaching second grade.
We're heading into the tail end of the school year,
and this week I got a new student. Fresh from the
Florida sun coast, this boy smells like he slept with
fish. He wears the same clothes at least three days in
a row, and his shoes don't match. His smile is one of
the sweetest I've ever seen, but I don't think he owns
a toothbrush. I processed all the necessary paperwork
so he will get free breakfast and lunch, but I worry
about dinner. He seems so grateful, so trusting. And
yet I feel myself pulling away from him.

He's a migrant worker's kid. He probably won't
be with us long. Getting to know him seems pointless. He'll just move on to another teacher in another

school. Then I feel the pricking of my spirit by the One who resides within. *You're the one with whom I'm entrusting him today. Love him as your own.*

Is it unfortunate this child was born to parents whose jobs change with the seasons? Yes. Is it a co-incidence that today he is in my class? No. I have something to offer him. If I keep my eyes and heart open, I will know what it is.

The poor have received a special blessing from God. They are rich in faith and heirs to the king-dom. Can I be a blessing to him as well? I hope so. I hold him closer to me than I hold those who sleep in warm beds and eat hot meals with their families. I let him know he is loved and considered and wor-thy of attention. And then six weeks later he is gone from my class. I wonder who God chose for his next teacher.

FINAL THOUGHT: Be a blessing and you will be blessed.

Father God, I pray for Your love and compassion to flow through me to all my students.

Show family affection to one another with brotherly love. Outdo one another in showing honor.

ROMANS 12:10

ONE-UPMANSHIP

I'm not real good at creating bulletin boards. When I'm finished with them, they never quite look like what I had in mind. I step back, cock my head to one side, squint my left eye, and ensure that it basically makes sense. I love words, so my bulletin boards are usually filled with straightforward information. Generally, I'm quite comfortable with my lack of artistic flair, but when I walk into the classroom of a teacher who clearly minored in art, my confidence plummets. This is definitely not an arena in which I can compete.

But competition rules the day. Now it seems teachers are encouraged to show one another up by their students' achievements. The number of As, Bs, and Fs you enter into the grading system earns you either praise or punishment. Unfortunately, some teachers assign grades in ways that may be questionable and sometimes not honorable. I don't want to compete with that.

Is it ever OK to try and outdo one another? Are the beautiful bulletin boards and enviable As all part of friendly competition? It's tempting to think so, but we're supposed to treat one another with brotherly love, not cutthroat rivalry. Let's compete for who shows more honor to students, parents, colleagues, and administrators. Let's treat one another at least as well as we treat ourselves. You would not intentionally dishonor yourself, so strive to treat everyone else with honor. This is a competition in which we can all win.

FINAL THOUGHT: Don't boast in your honor. Let others praise you when they see honor exemplified in your life.

Jesus, remind me not to promote the spirit of competition amongst my colleagues except in showing honor.

May you be strengthened with all power, according to His glorious might, for all endurance and patience, with joy giving thanks to the Father, who has enabled you to share in the saints' inheritance in the light.

COLOSSIANS 1:11-12

SECOND WIND

When I watch my son run the 1600 during a track meet, I worry about him. He's worked hard to improve his qualifying time: he's learned how to breathe correctly, he eats more protein and less simple sugars, and he pushes himself past his limits a little more every day. But as my eyes follow his gait around the striped ellipse, I see him wrestle for breath at the beginning of the final lap. His usually pale cheeks, now rose red, show the strain his pounding feet create. *He's not going to make it,* I worry. *He's going to slow to a walk.* I sit in the stands and pray that he finishes the race running and not walking. Maybe he doesn't practice enough. Maybe I need to make sure he eats better. Maybe he's just not built for running.

I have these same thoughts about myself when we

enter the fourth lap of the school year. Can I keep moving? I can see the finish line, but I'm bone weary, and it seems just out of my reach. In my mind I review what I've done to build endurance: I've stayed organized and prepared my lessons in advance. I've taken time off when I've needed it. And yet the final-lap strain flushes my cheeks, and my breathing becomes shallow. At the end of some school years, I wonder if I'm still cut out for this job.

What is the foundation of our endurance and strength? The only reliable source is our relationship with Christ. He enables us to walk the path marked out for us. His strength fills us better than any earthly nutrient, and His power recharges us better than any time off. This truth fuels me to keep putting one foot in front of the other. I will sprint and not hobble to the finish line.

 FINAL THOUGHT: Endurance comes from deep inside. Give thanks for it when it does.

Thank You, Jesus, for giving me the strength to endure.

All who are under the yoke as slaves must regard their own masters to be worthy of all respect, so that God's name and His teaching will not be blasphemed. And those who have believing masters should not be disrespectful to them because they are brothers, but should serve them better, since those who benefit from their service are believers and dearly loved.

1 TIMOTHY 6:1–2

WORKING FAVORITES

Nepotism. Not a nice word in some circles. They say it isn't what you know, but *who* you know that matters. I once taught at a school where the principal hired both her daughters. The rest of us wondered if we'd ever have a chance to gain her approval. We feared that these precious children of the principal wouldn't have to work as hard as we did. Would they come in late and leave early? Would they take days off without suffering an interrogation? Would parent complaints be swatted away without a thought? We wondered, but we didn't have to wonder for long.

Within the first grading period, it was obvious the

princesses intended to work harder for the queen than any of the rest of us. They came in early and left late. They didn't miss a day of school. And they handled parent complaints with the diplomacy of UN negotiators. I wanted to be just like them. They certainly had the principal's love, but they also had her respect. And suddenly *nepotism* didn't seem like such a bad thing.

As children of God we are sons and daughters of the King! And nepotism certainly rules in His kingdom. He uses us to accomplish His will on earth. Whether we're assigned to work for another brother or sister or someone outside the kingdom, our ultimate boss is the Lord. And out of our love for Him, our hands work diligently. We'll come in early and stay late. We'll make sure our work has the mark of quality on it. And who knows? Someone outside the kingdom may want to be just like us.

FINAL THOUGHT: Working for the King is a full-time job with incredible, unmatched benefits! Strive to always do your best.

My King, I bow before You in humble service. Bless the work of my hands.

*We proclaim Him, warning and teaching everyone
with all wisdom, so that we may present everyone
mature in Christ. I labor for this, striving with
His strength that works powerfully in me.*

COLOSSIANS 1:28–29

GROWING UP

I loved teaching middle school. Call me crazy, but
watching sixth graders enter like babies, turn into
scattered seventh graders, and finally leave as arrogant eighth graders made me smile. The hormonal
rush of young adolescents cluttering the hallways,
the lunch room, and the bus ramp is more than most
people can stand, even parents. But those of us who
love these "incorrigibles" work hard to help them
grow up before they leave for high school.

By the tail end of middle school, we've begun to
see this miraculous transformation we call *maturity*
begin to take place. Those who started out fearfully
disorganized now turn in their work on time on a
regular basis. Those whose handwriting resembled
chicken scratch now write in a more decipherable

code. Those whose personal-hygiene habits rivaled those of a caged animal finally stop offending noses at their passing. We teach; they learn. It's a beautiful thing! The transformation can be dramatic and inspires us to continue year after year. There is no time of life when the process of maturing is so obvious and fast paced as in middle school.

My early discipleship felt like that. I started out awfully naive and unpolished, easily swayed by new teachings, and legalistic. My mentors and teachers were patient with me, led by example, and encouraged me during a time when I must have seemed hopeless. I've grown because of it. I'm grateful for the people God placed in my life to smooth my hair, pick lint off of my suit, and present me equipped to serve in the kingdom. May I always be motivated to do the same for every child who crosses my path.

FINAL THOUGHT: Imagine you are preparing each of your students to stand before a college board, a job interviewer, or Christ Himself. What can you do to get each one ready?

Lord, continue to help me mature so that someday I may stand before You unashamed.

First of all, then, I urge that petitions, prayers, intercessions, and thanksgivings be made for everyone, for kings and all those who are in authority, so that we may lead a tranquil and quiet life in all godliness and dignity.

I Timothy 2:1–2

The Most Important Duty

One more thing. If they ask me to do one more thing, I'm going to scream! I sat in the professional-development workshop, arms crossed, with a skeptical scowl on my face, and I waited. I waited for the workshop leader to utter those words, the ones that are like a red cape to a bull—"Incorporate this into your routine, and it will make your teaching day so much easier." At this point in the year, the only thing that will make my teaching day easier is for it to end earlier. Unfortunately, the end-of-the-year checklist looms, and my day fills with duties and activities that bring the year to a soft close. Why does it then feel so hard?

The stick that broke the camel's back was just

that—a stick—one small, virtually weightless stick. The overburdened animal, although bred for pack work, couldn't take another step when one more stick was added to its already weighed-down aching back. He collapsed, just as I believed I would if one more person asked me to do one more thing. I just needed some peace, and I knew this workshop leader couldn't give me that.

When we reach the end of our rope, we look for the one thing that will bring us rest and relief. What would happen if we looked for it first instead? God encourages us to pray first for ourselves and for those with whom we work. We can begin each day, even the last days of school, with prayer and then walk through each of those days with a greater measure of peace. Yes, it's one more thing to do, but it's the first and most important thing to do each day.

FINAL THOUGHT: When you only use prayer as a last resort, you miss its potential for bringing peace to your life.

Lord, fill my day with peace!

*He will repay each one according to his works: eternal
life to those who by patiently doing good seek for glory,
honor, and immortality; but wrath and indignation to
those who are self-seeking and disobey the truth,
but are obeying unrighteousness.*

ROMANS 2:6–8

AWARDS

Awards ceremonies certainly have changed. As I sat in
a metal-back chair in the "cafetorium," I watched each
eighth grader receive a myriad of awards that exalted
mediocrity. Everyone received a good-attendance certificate, a worthy-effort certificate, and many received
the coveted honor-roll certificate as long as they didn't
get more than two Cs. I could see the standards plum-
met from my front-row seat.

We used to honor excellence. We used to laud
character traits. We used to sing the praises of those
who did well, not those who hoped to do well someday. It's hard to get excited about end-of-the-year
awards when the benchmarks have moved to the
end of the line.

One of the last to leave the stage was a girl from my language-arts class. Kara always followed directions, turned in her work on time, and maintained an A average. She was kind, considerate, and included others whenever she got the chance. Yet she left the stage with three pieces of paper that didn't recognize any of her accomplishments. When she stopped to accept her yearbook from me, I stood and hugged her. "Thank you for bringing excellence to my class this year. I wish I had a hundred students just like you." Her shy smile was my reward. I just wish I could have given her more.

What the world values and what God values are often two different things. Look for those eternal traits in your students. Applaud those who go above and beyond. Reward those who pursue excellence. Let God take care of the rest.

FINAL THOUGHT: Make sure your students know what you value. Point them always to their eternal reward.

Jesus, help me to recognize and honor excellence whenever possible, and do not let me be swayed from Your values by the pressures of the world.

For we don't dare classify or compare ourselves with some who commend themselves. But in measuring themselves by themselves and comparing themselves to themselves, they lack understanding.

2 CORINTHIANS 10:12

WHERE DO YOU STAND?

We stopped administering nationally standardized tests a number of years ago in favor of state standardized tests. The goal was to be able to determine how equitable the education was from district to district in our own state. Well, we certainly found that out, but we sacrificed knowing where we stood in comparison to other states. Comparing ourselves to ourselves hasn't quite instilled confidence in our education system. There's some fear when it comes to finding out where you stand in the grand scheme of things, and in this age of accountability educators are scared.

On the classroom level we get a little uneasy when one third-grade teacher's class does exponentially better than another third-grade teacher's class. But what if we compared the outstanding class to all other third-grade classes in the country and discovered it performed at the bottom of the heap? Standing tall as the king of the hill is a matter of perspective. It all depends on how high your hill is.

We stand before a mighty God, the King of the hill, and we are dwarfed in His presence. We do not dare compare ourselves or our performance to a Holy God. Yet when we waste time measuring ourselves against others who are just as fallible as we are, we learn nothing. We may even end up with a false sense of superiority. We should, instead, give Him our best, not worrying what other people do and not spinning our wheels with useless comparisons.

FINAL THOUGHT: God doesn't grade on a curve—His standards are set in stone. Your performance is not measured against anyone else's. It's just you and God.

Heavenly Father, Your standards are the only ones that matter. Help me to work to please You alone.

But avoid irreverent, empty speech, for this will
produce an even greater measure of godlessness.
And their word will spread like gangrene.

2 TIMOTHY 2:16–17

POWERFUL WORDS

Everyone seems a little loose toward the end of the year. They're not working as hard. They lounge a little longer, and they saunter down the hallways. The kids are a little louder, and the discipline a little lax. Some teachers have already begun to pack up their rooms, while others haven't given it a thought. They're all in various stages of saying good-bye to this school year.

The problem with the coming end of school is that too many teachers are coming to the end of themselves. Throughout the year there has been the usual amount of grumbling and gossip. But now it seems the relaxed atmosphere of the last two weeks of school has loosened tongues even more. Teachers are not as mindful of the things they say, and words slip to reveal their worn and weary souls. Spoken with disregard, the grumbling can spread discontent to otherwise contented individuals. They may complain about the principal, the parents, and the pupils, no matter who is listening.

Now more than ever you need to reject the onslaught of complaint. Turn away from it, so you can navigate the last days of the school year with visible dignity. Fill your heart with gratitude so that you are protected against the barrage of rants. Let your words come from a heart filled with honor and not bitterness. Walk this way, and other teachers will follow.

FINAL THOUGHT: Discontent is an infectious disease, but you can cure it with thanksgiving.

Lord, You have been faithful all year in guarding my ears and closing my lips when necessary. Get me through these last couple of weeks with dignity and honor.

Now we want each of you to demonstrate the same diligence for the final realization of your hope, so that you won't become lazy, but imitators of those who inherit the promises through faith and perseverance.

HEBREWS 6:11–12

THE BEGINNING OF THE END

Our end-of-the-year countdowns can be pretty elaborate. One year I had ten helium balloons tied in a bunch. Every day one of my students would get to pop a balloon. This activity was usually met with rip-roaring applause. It was difficult to get students settled back down to work, but I knew how much they looked forward to it every day. I didn't want to ruin their fun—or mine.

It's time for the final countdown. It's OK to feel relief that the end of the year is almost here. You may feel a renewed sense of hope that entices you with promised rest. You have a well-deserved sense of accomplishment, and you may be tempted to sit back and wait for the end to come.

But there's still much to do. You're ready for the

year to be over, but you're not done yet. Your hope doesn't lie in reaching the last day of school. It lies in your salvation and the privilege of sharing it with as many people as possible. Stay focused. Stay alert. Keep watch for an opportunity to share that hope. You're running out of time!

FINAL THOUGHT: Something to add to your end-of-the-year checklist: share your faith with someone you encounter at your school!

Father God, thank You for the hope that only comes from You. Empower and embolden me to share that hope with others.

*For even in Thessalonica you sent [gifts] for my need
several times. Not that I seek the gift, but I seek the
fruit that is increasing to your account. But I have
received everything in full, and I have an abundance.*

PHILIPPIANS 4:16–18

The Gift

With the end of the school year comes gifts. There's
something special about the fact that some parents go
out of their way to show their appreciation. Elementary teachers tend to receive more gifts than secondary teachers, but no matter how many or how few,
the thought behind them means something. These
gifts are rarely given out of obligation or compulsion.
They're given out of a true sense of gratitude. They
may not all be original, but they're always welcomed.

Some parents get creative with their gift giving.
No teacher mouse pads or miniatures for them! I've
received movie tickets for two, a box of copy paper,
and even a membership in the plant-of-the-month
club. Some of the most precious things I've received
have been personalized handmade gifts from the

students themselves. But the most treasured gifts I've gotten weren't the gifts at all, but the cards that accompanied them.

I've kept every card and note I've received over the years. The gifts themselves may have ended up being given to charity or sold at a garage sale (one can only have so many I Love Teaching coffee mugs), but the words of sentiment are kept close to my heart in a keepsake box. The words tell the story of a life I impacted. They take me back to a precious toothless grin or an exuberant class clown. They remind me why I went into teaching in the first place and motivate me to continue answering this call.

Jesus is the Word, and He is God's gift to us. All we have to do is accept the gift. When parents offer me their gifts and words, all I have to do is receive them.

FINAL THOUGHT: Gifts are for giving, and words are some of life's most precious gifts. What words can you offer parents about their child that would be received with a grateful heart?

I can't thank You enough, God, for the gifts You shower on me in the form of these students who will soon no longer be in my care. Open my eyes to the gifts I can leave with them as we part ways.

*You must speak what is consistent
with sound teaching.*

TITUS 2:1

SAY WHAT YOU MEAN, AND
MEAN WHAT YOU SAY

I teach creative writing as an on-line course. When we discuss character development and dialogue, I tell students that one of the most common beginning writing mistakes is when a character says or does something not consistent with who he or she is. For example, if the main character is an arrogant, back-talking, backwoods man in his forties, he wouldn't say something like, "Excuse me, ma'am, pardon my intrusion." Or when a young woman, born with a silver spoon in her mouth and winner of the Miss America pageant, steals a stranger's car and takes her friends out to knock down mailboxes with baseball bats, it's not believable. It's not credible, because it's not consistent with the character.

Kids can smell inconsistency a mile away, and they're quite willing to point it out. When you, a mild-mannered educator, suddenly throw a temper tantrum (because you got no sleep the night before), it scares them into humbled, silent submission. They look at you like you just landed on this planet. You acted out of character, and they don't know what to think.

God is immutable and so is His Word. His actions and His speech are completely consistent with His character. His principles, wisdom, and commandments all reflect who He is. We know what to expect from Him. As we walk in God's principles and obey His commandments, our students see who we are. If we want to be believable to them, trustworthy and respected, then we had better be consistent.

FINAL THOUGHT: Your character reflects that of your Creator; make sure it's a true reflection.

Heavenly Father, may I always reflect and glorify You.

DAY 174

*Instead you should say, "If the Lord wills,
we will live and do this or that." But as it is,
you boast in your arrogance. . . . So, for the person
who knows to do good and doesn't do it, it is a sin.*

JAMES 4:15–17

THE LEAST AMOUNT OF REGRETS

"Don't worry about it. Next year will be better," Susan comforted her friend. "After all, you can only do what you can do."

Janet pondered this possibility. She measured the promise of next year against what she perceived as failure from this year. She'd never found time to call every parent with positive news like she'd planned. Maybe if she had, Jeremy wouldn't have been so difficult to handle. As she considered the coming end of the school year, she wondered why the hope for next year didn't soften her regret.

We try to do a good job, but sometimes things fall through the cracks. It's understandable, but that doesn't mean it's OK. Some things are too important to dismiss. As we think about what we were and weren't able to accomplish this year, we shouldn't adopt the "Oh well, better luck next time" attitude. If there's anything that causes you to feel an inkling of regret, stop, listen to the Spirit that prods you, and do the very thing you've been putting off. Even if it's on the last day of school, do what needs to be done.

No one knows what tomorrow will bring. We might assume there will be a next month or a next year, but there's no guarantee. What we don't do to-day, we'll regret tomorrow. Do what you can as each opportunity arises. You may not get another chance.

FINAL THOUGHT: Scarlett O'Hara was wrong. Today is the only day that matters.

Lord, what have I neglected to do this year? Show me so that I can make it right.

If the trumpet makes an unclear sound, who will prepare for battle? In the same way, unless you use your tongue for intelligible speech, how will what is spoken be known? . . . Therefore the person who speaks in [another] language should pray that he can interpret.

1 CORINTHIANS 14:8–9, 13

MAKE IT MAKE SENSE

I had a whole year to learn how to communicate more effectively with Natalie, a deaf student in my fifth-grade class. She wore two hearing aids and read lips like a pro, but at times my using sign language would have really helped her understand our math lessons better. I tried, but I just couldn't get the hang of it. I got more giggles out of Natalie than understanding.

The only way I could make sure Natalie understood the lesson was to stand right in front of her and speak clearly. That way if she couldn't hear me, she could read my lips. I had to make sure that when another student offered a comment I repeated it for Natalie. I also tried to offer instruction through more visual than auditory channels. I used computer-projected images, instructional handouts, and videos to teach a concept. I organized learning partners so one could help the other whenever necessary. All this to ensure Natalie learned in my class.

And then something amazing happened.

At the tail end of the year, I spied commotion in the back of the class during a quiet learning activity. As I approached the small group gathered around their graph paper, I saw a flurry of fingers—both signing and writing. Natalie sat at the center of the group as if holding court. She was the one explaining the activity to her team members, and they were responding, partly in sign language. Somehow I'd created an environment that enabled Natalie to both learn and teach. How gratifying to finally see that my diligence had paid off.

 FINAL THOUGHT: Take whatever steps necessary to ensure things make sense to kids. You may think they can't hear you, but when you least expect it, they'll show you they were listening all along.

You are the Master Communicator, Lord. Show me how to speak in a language all my students will understand.

*Even if I am poured out as a drink offering
on the sacrifice and service of your faith, I am glad
and rejoice with all of you. In the same way you also
should rejoice and share your joy with me.*

PHILIPPIANS 2:17–18

THE END IS NEAR

Just as spring comes in like a lion and goes out like
a lamb, so the school year begins with a shout and
ends with a whimper. We are so weary by the end
that just getting out of bed in the morning feels like
lifting three times our body weight. There's nothing
left. No more lessons to plan. No more phone calls
to make. No more papers to grade. We are empty
vessels that once carried the finest wine. There's not
a drop left to pour out—and yet our students raise
their glasses and ask for more. Why do they still
come to us for more? Because they know we'll give
it to them.

Good teachers give 100 percent of themselves to
their work. Great teachers give 110 percent. How do
we give more than we have? We steal bits and pieces

from other parts of our lives to make up the difference. Sometimes our families suffer. Sometimes our health suffers. Sometimes our relationship with God suffers. But we don't mind the sacrifice. We know it's necessary. What rewards could possibly warrant such sacrifices?

God delights when He hears that another of His children has chosen to return home. He offered His only Son as a living sacrifice for that very possibility. Does one human life warrant such a sacrifice? In God's eyes, yes. When Jesus hung on the cross, His last words sounded like our own. "It is finished!" But even though his earthly ministry ended, His impact had only just begun.

FINAL THOUGHT: The end of the year is the beginning of your eternal impact. What you poured into those students will continue to be poured out in the lives of countless others.

Lord Jesus, thank You for your sacrifice! And thank You for allowing me to share in Your sacrifice in small ways.

If I have [the gift of] prophecy,
and understand all mysteries and all knowledge,
and if I have all faith, so that I can move mountains,
but do not have love, I am nothing.

1 CORINTHIANS 13:2

KNOW-IT-ALLS

The education students I teach are obsessed with completing the content. We place a great deal of emphasis on meeting high academic standards. We have a variety of hoops through which preservice teachers must jump to be certified for the job of teaching. We've created rubrics for every feasible purpose and checklists to observe every possible skill. We expect students to navigate the learning landscape using cutting-edge technology. But my job includes more than recording the grades they earn on any given assignment. It includes getting a glimpse into their hearts.

Education is all about relationship. You can know the content, but if you don't know the kids in the seats, your message falls on deaf ears. There is a perceivable and necessary distance between student and teacher, but we should never be so disconnected that we don't know the inner workings and struggles of the students assigned to us.

Whenever we remember a favorite teacher, it isn't because of her knowledge alone. We remember that she cared about us! For some students we may be the only one in their lives who cares. Be remembered because you knew your students well enough to change their lives. As they leave this year to go on to other teachers, they'll remember you because you remembered them first.

FINAL THOUGHT: She loves me; she loves me not. Make sure your students know you love them.

Thank You, God, for knowing me, remembering me, and loving me.

DAY 178

My son, don't forget my teaching, but let your heart
keep my commands; for they will bring you
many days, a full life, and well-being.

PROVERBS 3:1–2

ALL DRESSED UP AND
NO PLACE TO GO

Having lived in Florida during my adult life, I never
thought about what it can take to get children ready
to play outside in January until we moved to Colorado. The many layers of clothing I helped them
into matched the number of arguments they offered
in return. Didn't they understand the goal of stay-
ing warm? Actually, they didn't. They were born in
Florida, so Colorado winters were a novelty to them.
My mother-knows-best commandments usually won
out, and they dutifully put on wool socks over cotton
ones inside boots, warm-up pants under snow pants,
a long-sleeve shirt and a sweater under their down-
filled coats, hats that covered their ears and scarves
to protect their necks and chests, and thin-fingered
gloves under thick, waterproof mittens.

I admit I overdressed them, but at least I knew they could play out in the snow for hours without getting cold. The bright Colorado sun forced the layers off after an hour or so, and by the time they came inside, they were only wearing a sweater, snow pants, and the waterproof mittens. It makes sense to over-prepare. That way you'll never be caught unaware.

Sometimes we've packed so much into the school year that we envision our students about to burst at the seams like the gluttonous child in *Willie Wonka and the Chocolate Factory*. They may not need all we give them, and they won't use everything they've learned in their future jobs. But you can rest in the fact that you filled them up with truth and not hot air. As long as that's the case, they'll be able to take what they need for where they're going.

FINAL THOUGHT: No one ever regrets giving more. The only regret comes when we don't give enough.

Thank You, Lord, for preparing me for this job. And thank You for the privilege of helping You prepare these students for their own futures.

*And the King will answer them, "I assure you:
Whatever you did for one of the least of these
brothers of Mine, you did for Me."*

MATTHEW 25:40

WHO'D I DO THIS FOR?

No one said, "Thank you." Then again, hardly anyone says, "Please," "God bless you," or "May I help you?" anymore either. Maybe you went out of your way this year to work with a struggling student three days a week before school. Maybe you complimented a particularly shy young lady privately to help boost her self-esteem. Maybe you stopped a bully from extorting lunch money from some of your meeker students. Maybe you went to bat for a parent who couldn't seem to get her case heard by the principal. Maybe you stood up for a colleague wrongly accused. Yet no one said, "Thank you."

Underappreciation is a common complaint of educators. At the end of the year, many teachers reevaluate their jobs. Was it all worth it? Are the poor working conditions, problem students and parents, inadequate communication and collaboration between colleagues, and societal blame worth the miniscule paycheck? For some it isn't, and they're tempted to leave.

We're looking for praise in all the wrong places from all the wrong people. Did you work extra hard with a struggling student so he would say thank you? Did you stop the bully so the victim's parents would thank you? Sometimes they do express gratitude, but don't let that be your motivation. When you defend the defenseless, protect the unprotected, love the unlovable, or bear with the unbearable, you do it for those in need. You do it for Jesus.

And Jesus says, "Thank you!"

FINAL THOUGHT: What you did this year for students didn't go unnoticed. God sees you even when no one else does.

As long as I'm working for You, God, I can do whatever is asked of me with no earthly thanks at all. Your praise means everything to me.

Day 180

May our Lord Jesus Christ Himself and God our Father,
who has loved us and given us eternal encouragement
and good hope by grace, encourage your hearts and
strengthen you in every good work and word.

2 Thessalonians 2:16–17

Benediction

I watched as an entire congregation laid their hands on the heads of one small family about to return to the mission field. Those who weren't close enough raised their hands toward them and spoke words over them in blessing. The road ahead would be difficult and fraught with challenges and obstacles yet unseen. They'd been down this road before, but it's different every time. Their church family pours blessing upon them as they walk forward in faith.

It's the last day of school. It's a day of celebration. Not because you watched some of your students walk across a stage and receive their diplomas, but because you finished a difficult year. We celebrate beginnings and endings. We need prayer from start to finish. We know this end is just the beginning of

360

preparation for the next school year. And I'm here to pour blessings upon your head. Like precious oil, let it cover your hair from roots to tips. Feel it flow down your neck and then slowly cover your body.

Lord, see your faithful servants and grant them the blessing of peace for a job well done. Thank You for protecting them throughout this school year. Thank You for blessing the work of their hands. Thank You for revealing Yourself when they felt completely alone. Provide rest for their souls as they prepare for this next year. Stand with them; stand for them; stand beside them as they take each step toward the fulfillment of Your will. They have been a blessing. Bless them abundantly and exceedingly more than they could ever fathom so Your name may be praised!

FINAL THOUGHT: Let the peace of God be with you always.

Lord, thank You for granting me exactly what I needed every day to do the work You prepared just for me.

Vicki Caruana is an educator at both the high school and college level. She is a professor for the college of education at St. Petersburg College and a learning specialist at The Collegiate High School in St. Petersburg, Florida. She has written more than twenty books about education for parents and teachers and is a frequent educational and home-schooling conference speaker. Vicki authored the best-selling book *Apples & Chalkdust: Inspirational Stories & Encouragement for Teachers* (Honor, 1998). For more encouragement for teachers, visit her Web site at www.vickicaruana.blogspot.com.